T0345314

THE GODDESS

THE GODDESS

MYTHS OF THE GREAT MOTHER

Christopher Fee &
David Leeming

REAKTION BOOKS

To our mothers, grandmothers, daughters, granddaughters, sisters, aunts and nieces: goddesses all. David sees the faces of the Goddess in Pam, Margaret, Juliet, Julia, Morgan, Brooklyn, Emilia and Margaret. Chris traces his devotion to the Goddess to Allison, Emma, Chandler, Emmy Lou, Martha, Betty, Catherine, Sandie, Pat, Bernice, Ann, Carmen, Charley, Arrielle and Alyssa.

Published by Reaktion Books Ltd
Unit 32, Waterside
44–48 Wharf Road
London N1 7UX, UK
www.reaktionbooks.co.uk

First published 2016

Printed and bound in Great Britain by TJ International, Padstow, Cornwall

A catalogue record for this book is available from the British Library

ISBN 978 1 78023 509 7

Contents

Seated goddess with a child, from the Hittite Empire period,
c. 14th–13th century BCE, found in Central Anatolia.

INTRODUCTION

The Many Guises of the Goddess

For time out of mind, an ancient goddess reigned supreme, and the fertile soil of the land beneath her feet bespoke her immeasurable fecundity. Long ages she ruled, and many were her worshippers. Then, 5,000 years ago or more, perhaps in the region where steppe meets sea in the great central land mass where Asia and Europe conjoin, tribes began to shift and migrate, and their movements were to transform this goddess forever. These peoples began to move south and east into the Indian subcontinent, down into what is now Iran, up to the Baltic, west along the European coast of the Mediterranean to the Atlantic, and even across the ocean to lands past the horizon. Over thousands of years and miles, these people we often call Indo-Europeans divided into many groups and settled in many regions, and ever the goddess travelled with them; always she transformed to suit her people, her face ever reflecting the needs and desires of her children. The demands of her peoples could be harsh, however, and thus over time this goddess – so often beautiful with the love of her followers – could be seen to be terribly transformed, and love sometimes turned to fear among many of her worshippers. The face of the Earth Mother – comely and resplendent with the abundance of her life-giving womb – alternated with a grimmer guise, her maternal, loving laughter at times replaced with the gruesome grimace of a skull's head. Raining death from above, many are the masks of this Great Goddess, who combines her ancient love of life with a terrible taste for death.

Sometimes such a fearsome face of the goddess reveals little of her ancient life-affirming form; her mask seems then altered permanently as she assumes some of the more terrifying attributes of a male counterpart. For example, as the Indian Rudra – the Vedic god of death and ill-fortune – slowly becomes Shiva, 'the auspicious one', in the later Hindu pantheon, his destructive powers and terrible attributes are transferred to his consort, once a mother goddess, who shifts from suckling nurturer to demonic destroyer. Many of her Indian sisters are associated to this day with disease and the destructive forces of nature, shorn of their most natural powers as new faces of death are thrust upon them. Meanwhile, where the erstwhile Indo-European goddess met her sisters from the Near East, she partook sometimes of their identities, adding new and exotic faces to her collection of masks. Moreover, where this most ancient goddess has fallen beneath the shadow of the jealous One God of Judaism, Christianity or Islam, she is almost utterly bereft. Often marginalized as a virgin vessel or as a destructive whore, in either case this timeless Mother and Destroyer often is robbed almost entirely of either identity, of her autonomy and of her paired powers of production and destruction.

Beneath even the most terrible of the Destroyer masks of the goddess, however, we may sometimes capture a glimpse of an earlier beauty, evidence of a more benign and life-giving identity; often this face is manifested through the sexual abandon which so often links lust with death. Indeed, sometimes this goddess counters the life-giving force of her still-ample hips with the blood-reddened tip of her life-taking spear; in such guises she reeks of both sex and decay. The goddess multiplies herself, for instance, to appear as a number of Destroyer demigoddesses who serve as handmaids to the Scandinavian All-father. These shield-maidens – called the Valkyries – are fickle with their favours; they may grant glory and victory to a man time and again, only to betray him to a spear's point at the last. The Valkyries are thought to be virgins, but they are at the same time the little sisters of Freyja. This goddess of fertility, fecundity and lust makes room in her bed for all the races of gods and elves, and yet paradoxically fills the benches of her hall with a share of Odin's battle-slain. The Irish Morrígan likewise combines a burning and insatiable appetite for physical love with the cruel and pitiless sensibilities of a death goddess. Thus the Morrígan, denied the sexual gratification she craves that only Cúchulainn – the greatest of Éire's heroes – can provide, uses her destructive powers against him when he spurns her advances, and mocks him as he dies. The Morrígan is half-sister to Medb, queen of the demigods of Ireland, whose bloodlust is only equalled by her indefatigable prowess in bed. Many heroes have fought that gentler battle, and it is only in her arms that a man may claim the right to call himself king.

The faces of God and Goddess always reflect the souls of the people who worship them. The various transformations of the face of the goddess of these related mythologies – and the patterns we may discern in these transformations throughout thousands of years, traversing thousands of miles, across a wide spectrum of descendant cultures – have much to teach us about the transformation of relevant cultures and values. The emergence, dominance and subsequent subordination or erasure of powerful female figures of worship in this set of mythologies is an overarching theme of this book, and this theme has never been more relevant than it is today. The distant ancestors of the dominant cultures of India, Iran and Europe began their migrations from western Asia 5,000 years ago, and various tribes from this group spawned the classical civilizations of the lands they colonized. All of contemporary Western civilization, therefore, traces some large cultural debt to these ancient ancestors, and thus related ancient transformations regarding the role of women and of conceptions of feminine divinities are of immediate and urgent interest to those who have a stake in modern gender roles.

In recent years, it has been a popular belief that the peoples we are describing, the hordes that swept, often violently, into Europe, parts of the Near East and India from western Asia between 3,000 and 5,000 years ago, were dominated by the worship of a patriarchal, militaristic Sky God, a male king of gods who supplanted the Earth Mother of the indigenous Europeans. An unfortunate result of this generalization has been the assumption that the goddess long had been subordinated completely in that ancient pantheon, and that there is thus little of interest to say about her development. The story of the goddess, however, is a tale of resilience, and the mythology of these invaders was more dynamic and multifaceted than this reductive model suggests. The goddess, even repressed, is a force to be reckoned with, and many powers and attributes are associated with her.

During the period of migration and invasion she was always with her people, undergoing a series of transmutations in the crucibles of changing societies.

Characteristics of minor goddesses from the Celtic, Germanic, Iranian and Indian traditions, for instance, vibrantly illustrate shifts in cultural values over time regarding powerful, female divine forces. While many such figures appear in these mythologies, they tend to be marginalized, to have strictly defined roles, and to be manifestations of one facet of a larger, more recognizable goddess figure. Minor though they may seem, then, in reality these figures are phantom shadows of features of the great goddess who once dominated her realm. Contact with Christianity and with Islam transformed such figures in particularly interesting ways. For example, the scholar of Old English Helen Damico used the term 'Valkyrie reflex' to describe a trend in Old English Christian literature which renders the familiar Germanic battle demigoddesses into female saints and shield-maidens of Christ. Such minor goddesses recur throughout mythologies we will study, and actually represent shadowy reflections of feminized, archetypal destroyer deities.

In much of the later, literary mythology, we see again and again a false dichotomy between the patriarchal Sky God and the matriarchal Earth Goddess, and quite often the former takes on the protector/destroyer role while the latter is associated most closely with fertility. The minor goddesses belie this reductive understanding of the archetypal relationship between fertility and destruction, and it is an interesting comment on the cultures in question (and indeed, on our own) that the powerful feminine destroyer/protector is so often demonized or marginalized. Moreover, these mythologies provide a lot of good stories: such goddesses are still popularly associated with disease and elemental destruction in the south of India, for example, where tales, rituals and even comic books concerning them are extremely common. It is also particularly interesting that such figures in the Middle East were routinely demonized by Islam; further, the Irish and Germanic manifestations of these goddesses were transformed in similar ways by Christianity, and in fact have much in common with their eastern cousins. Such transmutations have much to teach us about ancient (and modern) conceptions and fears concerning the power of the female.

The following chapters address important issues concerning female agency and power in the various pantheons involved, associations which are perhaps most notable when destructive powers and terrible attributes have been assigned to female figures. Such identities might be interpreted either as the demonization of the feminine generally or as the assumption of power by the goddess; in fact, it might well represent a combination of these two cultural transformations.

The emphasis of this book is on the patterns of ways in which goddesses – as opposed to male deities – transform and evolve in the pantheons we examine, as well as on how such changes may be correlated with cultural and religious shifts. The Indian material is particularly significant because the earliest Sanskrit texts may well represent the most unadulterated mythic material available from the earliest of the traditions involved – this matter escaped being largely influenced by contact with Christianity or Islam, as more Western traditions have been. Our survey of the Iranian material focuses on the transformation of ancient sources in the context of Islam, and is valuable to any reader interested in conceptions of gender and power in that newer tradition. A study of the conflict and confluence of these systems is also a valuable counterpoint to any discussion of the transformation of earlier pagan material through its submergence in Christian culture. Our examination of the Middle Eastern and Mediterranean goddess traces the lines of confluence and influence between the Indo-European classical traditions and the ancient and wholly unrelated mythic material with which they came into contact. In our treatment of more western material – notably the Celtic and Germanic – we trace this Christian metamorphosis through the medieval period. These transformations have much to teach us about the genesis of modern European and American conceptions of gender and power and, indeed, raise the spectre of the cultural basis for rationalizations of colonialism in the early modern period.

Myths of the Great Mother describes the many and changing faces of the ancient Earth Goddess of the Indo-Europeans, noting in particular her peregrinations with her migrating children, the tribes which would develop the Indic, Iranian and European mythologies as we now know them. In particular, this work seeks to describe the shifting masks of the goddess and especially her vacillation between life-giver and life-taker, explaining what this ambivalence has to tell us about the relationship between production and destruction, between sex and death, and between power and agency in the relevant cultures. It is our hope that this examination of the many faces of the goddess may help to reflect and illuminate pertinent aspects of the relationship between our own culture and its ancient roots.

I

The Dawn of
the Indian Goddess

Genesis

Archaeological evidence indicates the presence of *Homo sapiens* in the Indian subcontinent from at least 75,000 BCE. The land was conducive to agricultural and urban development, and over the centuries such development took place to the extent that by 2600 BCE the area around the Indus River was home to one of the four great urban civilizations of the world, the others being Egypt, Mesopotamia and China. The Indus Valley, or Harappan, civilization was an advanced culture consisting of at least two major urban centres, Harappa and Mohenjo-daro, and as many as one thousand other cities and villages across an area that included what we know today as northeast Afghanistan, Pakistan and northwest India. The Indus Valley people used advanced brickwork for homes and public buildings; created water and irrigation systems; were adept at seal carving and bronze, copper, lead and tin work; and possessed a writing system – still undeciphered – for a language which scholars believe to have been a member of the Dravidian language family, of which many offshoots – for example Tamil and Telugu – are still spoken in southern India today.

What happened next in ancient India is disputed. The Vedic period, which takes its name from the Vedas, the sacred texts that eventually provided the basis for Hinduism, began in about 1500 BCE. There is strong feeling in India that the Vedic culture developed naturally from within India itself. The majority of scholars, however, subscribe to the theory that people once commonly called Aryans, and now generally called Indo-Iranians or simply Indo-Europeans, migrated into the subcontinent from the northwest in about 1500 BCE and brought with them a culture which mingled – in some cases by force – with the Harappan culture they encountered there. The primary support for this theory is the Indo-Iranian connection. It is argued that the so-called Aryans, speaking offshoots of a Central Asian-based proto-Indo-European language – the source for Greek, Latin and most of the European languages – moved into both Iran and India at about the same time, and brought certain traditions with them, including elements of the Indo-European language family that we find in ancient Indian Sanskrit and Iranian Farsi. This theory is further supported by the existence of common aspects shared by ancient Iranian and Indian religions: the god Mitra; the ritual drink 'soma' in the Vedas and 'haoma' in the Iranian sacred text the Avesta; and similar, clearly related – if sometimes opposing – terms for gods and demons. *Daevas* in the Iranian tradition are negative spirits, even false gods. In the Vedic period in India, *devas* are the younger gods sometimes in conflict with the older, somewhat negatively depicted *asuras*, whose Iranian cognates are the highly regarded *ahuras*, such as the high god Ahura Mazda. There are also descriptions in the most ancient of the Vedas, the Rig Veda, of the Battle of the Ten Kings, in which a tribe named the Bharatas was on the winning side. For those who subscribe to the Indo-European invasion theory, the Bharatas represent the Aryan invaders or migrants in conflict with the non-Aryan Harappans. Later, in the Sanskrit epic the *Mahabharata*, the Bharatas, under their emperor Bharata, were depicted as the conquerors of India. The official name of India in Hindi is Bhārata.

The Vedic period lasted until about 500 BCE. The continuing process of urbanization, the rise of Jainism and Buddhism, and the emergence of at least sixteen kingdoms (Mahajanapada, 'great realm') during the sixth to third centuries BCE led to a more pluralistic approach to religion and to an ascetic reform, or shamanic movement, and to the more popularly accessible texts, such as the original forms of the epics the *Ramayana* and the *Mahabharata*, that would later influence Hinduism. One of the most important of the Mahajanapada kingdoms was Magdaha, an important centre for Jainism and Buddhism as well as for the developing religion of Hinduism, bordered by the Ganges river. It was in part because of the rise of Buddhism and Jainism that the emerging classical Hinduism began to put less emphasis on the old Brahmanic rituals of Vedism. Classical Hinduism would develop fully during the rulership of the 'golden age' of the Gupta Empire between 320 and 650 CE, and would continue to thrive in many forms or schools, with Buddhism gradually losing ground to Hinduism in the late Gupta period. Muslim rule, beginning in 1100, saw conversions to Islam but also a further development of Hinduism.

Hinduism is the dominant religion of India today, although many would suggest that it, like Buddhism, is a philosophical system rather than a religion. It has no founder but has distinctive roots in the ancient Vedic traditions and rituals revealed in the Vedas themselves, as well as in related texts. An emphasis on Brahmanic rituals and authority – Brahmins being a priestly caste – is fairly consistent, as are the concepts of 'dharma' and 'karma'. To follow dharma is to assume certain duties and to adhere to certain rules affecting the overall way of life. Karma refers to the actions in one's life, actions that affect one's ultimate future, even – for some Hindus – one's reincarnation after death. Over the centuries, Hinduism has tended towards a *bhakti* (devotional) tradition in which sects have developed, usually centring on particular divinities, including the 'Great Goddess'. The myths of Hinduism seem to the outsider to be in conflict. Is the creator Vishnu, Brahma, Purusha or Prajapati? Did existence emerge from a cosmic egg or from the Creator's word or dismemberment? The answer to this conundrum lies in the fact that in the Vedic and Hindu traditions, the given myth speaks individually and metaphorically to a particular concept. At different times, and in different texts, various gods represent particular understandings of existence. The Vedic triad of Surya, Indra and Agni was eventually replaced by that of Brahma, Shiva and Vishnu, and still later, when interest in Brahma diminished, by the de facto triad of Shiva, Vishnu and the Great Goddess, Devi.

The concept of the triad remains essentially the same, having to do with the ultimate cycle of existence – inevitable creation, preservation and destruction – and pointing to an ultimate reality or Absolute, called Brahman by some, the neuter noun signifying the source of existence which is everywhere and nowhere. Brahman is the unknowable essence of all that is. In a practical sense, the unknown is experienced by devotion, most commonly to Shiva, Vishnu or Devi (Bhagavati), as various emanations of the Absolute or, for the most fervent worshippers of each – the Shaivites, the Vaishnavas and the Shaktas (worshippers of Devi-Shakti) – as the particular embodiment of the Absolute. The Shaktas, for example, argue that all things exist only because of Shakti, the cosmic energy of the Great Mother.

Goddesses, like all Indian deities, are embodiments of religious or philosophical knowledge. They appear in texts which are of divine origin (*śruti*) or texts somewhat less sacred but still religiously important (*smrti*). *Śruti* texts are said to have been transmitted directly by the deities to and 'heard' by seers or 'rishis'. These texts include the four Vedas, and the Brahmanas, the Aranyakas and the Upanishads, essentially extensions of the Vedas, much as the Talmud relates to the Torah in Judaism. *Smrti* texts include especially the Puranas and the two epics, the *Ramayana* and the *Mahabharata*. All of these texts – *śruti* and *smrti* – were transmitted orally in the ancient Sanskrit language, the language still used in Hindu rituals, much as Latin was, until recently, the language of the Catholic Church's liturgies. Sanskrit is a branch of the Indo-Iranian subfamily of the Indo-European languages. Its closest relative is the language of ancient Iran (Persia).

The *śruti* literature is the foundation of Hinduism. As completed and developed over time, the four Vedas – the Rig Veda, the Yajur Veda, the Sama Veda and the Atharva Veda – are central scriptures, each containing four basic elements: the Samhita, a collection of hymns and ritual formulae, or mantras, concerned with the natural world and deities; the Brahmana, or commentary on the given Veda; the Aranyaka, or meditative comment for the initiate to study on the Vedic rituals; and the Upanishad, collectively known also as Vedanta (Conclusion of the Vedas), spiritual explorations of ultimate questions such as Brahman, the unifying essence of the Universe, and Atman, the individual core in which Brahman can reside. The development of the Brahmanas, Aranyakas and Upanishads from the original Vedic texts reflects the change from the early nomadic Indo-Europeans to a more urbanized society in which more centralized Brahminic, or priestly, views prevailed. The *śruti* texts, especially the Rig Veda, the oldest of the Vedic texts, contain much of what we know of Vedic mythology. The Upanishads form the basis for what became a concern with salvation (moksha) and the almost monotheistic sense in schools such as Advayita Vedanta of Brahman as the reality embodied by all Hindu gods. The Upanishad tradition has continued into the Common Era and is important to Buddhists and Jains as well as Hindus. *Rig* means 'praise' in Sanskrit, and the Rig Veda is a collection of hymns and myths praising the gods. Indra is the most important of the Vedic gods. Others are the embodiment of Soma, Agni the sacrificial fire god, Surya the sun god and Varuna, another high god. Vishnu is here too, but of little importance. An early form of Shiva as Rudra is also present. Also central to the Rig Veda are several versions of creation.

The *Ramayana*, the *Mahabharata* and the Puranas are our primary sources for the myths of classical Hinduism. The two epics reflect a particular devotion to the god Vishnu and his avatars, Rama and Krishna. The *Mahabharata*, as it has ultimately developed, includes the great work the *Bhagavadgita*, which is a more popularly accessible extension of the spiritual explorations of the Upanishads. The *Gita* preaches the concept of dharma and celebrates the idea of the universal Brahman as revealed in Krishna-Vishnu. The Puranas, composed primarily during the Gupta period, tell the various myths of Hinduism beginning with the creation, and concentrate on stories of the greatest of the gods, especially Vishnu and Shiva. Among the Puranas are the Bhagavata and Vishnu Puranas, which centre on the avatars of Vishnu and especially the deeds of the avatar Krishna; the Shiva and Linga Puranas, which describe the characteristics and deeds of Shiva; and the Devi Bhagavata Purana, which concerns the Great Goddess Devi. The goddess in various forms is a constant and necessary component in both the *śruti* and *smrti* texts of Indian mythology and religion.

Faces of the Goddess

A large number of terracotta figures, dating from at least 3000 BCE and representing a full-breasted female with exposed genitals, have been found in the Indus Valley. These figures – which may remind us of the very famous and much earlier Palaeolithic 'Venuses' found at archaeological sites at Laussel in France and Willendorf in Austria – have led scholars to suggest that a mother goddess cult existed in the Indus Valley long before any possible arrival of Indo-Europeans in the subcontinent. There have been numerous theories surrounding this goddess. Perhaps the most widely accepted is that she is the earliest manifestation of what would become the great Indian goddess Devi, in her many forms. For devotees of Shaktism, for whom Devi or Shakti is the Absolute and the primary focus of devotion, the Indus Valley goddess was the first known manifestation, the first embodiment of the creative energy without which even Shiva and Vishnu are unrealized. The presence of archaeological evidence of a companion male deity to the goddess has led to further speculation. Worshippers of the god Shiva see this figure as Rudra, an early version of their manifestation of the Absolute. A terracotta image of particular interest to mythologists is one found in the ruins of the Indus Valley city of Mohenjo-daro of the goddess flanked by tigers. The association of the goddess with these powerful animals is reminiscent of the Great Goddess figurine from the Neolithic Çatalhöyük in Anatolia, who is also flanked by images of powerful feline figures (lions or tigers), or the goddess of Minoan Crete, who holds a snake in either hand. These goddesses all suggest power and even terror, as well as the nurturing that emerges naturally from the association of the female figure with birth and creation.

The Vedic goddesses are those whose identities are revealed in the *śruti* texts. These include Prithvi, Prakriti, Ushas, Vac or Sarasvati, and Aditi. The personification of Earth, Prithvi or Mata Prithvi (Mother Earth), or Dhra (Container of All Things), is a goddess with four arms and green skin. Her consort is Dyaus Pita (Father Sky), and she is said to be the mother of the Goddess of Dawn, Ushas. Prithvi is an early representation of the great Earth Goddess that we discover, for instance, in the Greek Gaia. Although Dyaus would essentially die out in later Hindu mythology, Prithvi remains. One myth tells how her womb became so full that she had to beg the creator for relief. In response, the creator made a beautiful woman, Death, whose tears became diseases and eased Prithvi's burden by destroying her offspring. The Prithvi myth, then, reflects the sense that the goddess, even as the manifestation of Life incarnate, is inevitably balanced by the reality of Death.

A development of the Dyaus-Prithvi construct is that of Purusha and Prakriti. Purusha, the primal being – the representation of spiritual reality and pure consciousness, who would be sacrificed and divided to become creation – is made manifest by the goddess Prakriti, material nature and the personification of the pure unconscious. Prakriti is the creative energy without which the god Purusha cannot be made known to the world. She is the essence of all goddesses, just as Purusha is the essence of all gods. As such, she is an early version of the concept of Shakti, that which makes the god appear. Prakriti, the World Mother, is at once intellect, ego, mind, creator, preserver and destroyer; the container, like Prithvi, of all things; and the prefiguration of the Hindu triad of Brahma the creator, Vishnu the preserver and Shiva the destroyer.

The Rig Veda depicts Ushas, the Goddess of Dawn, as a beautiful young woman riding her chariot across the sky. She is the daughter of the Sky, Dyaus, or in some versions of the creator god known as Prajapati, and she can sometimes be associated with Earth (*prithvi,* 'the vast one'). How Prajapati or Dyaus created her is not consistently revealed. Since Prajapati existed before all things, he must have been created ex nihilo – that is, from a part of himself, or by word of mouth. In any case, he mated with his daughter, who, in this instance, became more than Dawn; she became the Great Mother.

An early Rig Veda verse reveals that the Phallus of Heaven (Dyaus or Prajapati) reached out to his beautiful daughter Earth (Prithvi or Ushas) and had intercourse with her. Some of his spilled seed became words and rituals. In the Aitareya Brahmana, Prajapati approached his daughter as a stag and committed incest with her. In the Brihadaranyaka Upanishad, we return to Purusha, who created a female from himself and, taking various animal forms, mated with her.

All of this makes sense when we consider that, as Dawn, Ushas made the gods – represented sometimes, for instance, by the unapproachable sun god Surya – approachable. It is she who received the seed of the god as Prajapati or Purusha and made creation manifest. What was darkness or unconscious became approachable and conscious through her. Like Prithvi and Prakriti, she is the Mother

This late 19th-century print from Calcutta depicts Sarasvati, who manifests the face of the goddess as patroness of learning and of the arts, represented here by the manuscript of the Vedas at her side and the veena she is playing. The swan by her side is her traditional steed.

of Creation, a version of a larger goddess concept which will take form in classical Hinduism.

Beginning in Vedic times, speech – the word or sacred sound – was of special importance as a concept. Vac, whose name means 'word' and 'song', is related to Ushas and the myth of the creator's spilled seed, which became 'Word'. Whereas the speech of the divine is hidden, through Vac – through the goddess – it becomes manifest as the word, as, for instance, in the Vedas themselves. Vac, as depicted in the Upanishads, emerged from the god within – Atman. Once again, it is the goddess through whom the divine is realized.

Vac is sometimes the same as Sarasvati, who embodied wisdom and the arts and who later would be best known as the daughter of Brahma and still later as his wife. Sarasvati, whose name refers to water, was originally an ancient river goddess. She was also seen as one of the flames of the tongue of the Vedic fire of Agni and sometimes as his wife. In some Vedic hymns she is the wife of the Vedic king-god Indra. In the Upanishads she is Brahma's wife, Brahma having begun to replace Prajapati as creator. Sarasvati is often depicted dressed in white and sitting on a white lotus, signifying purity of truth. She has four arms, representing the four Vedas, and she carries four objects: a book representing the Vedas, a container of water representing creative and pure learning, a collection of crystals representing spirituality and a veena, a musical instrument, representing the arts. Even as Brahma gradually lost his importance, Sarasvati maintained hers.

Aditi, the 'endless' goddess, is eternity, unlimited space and time. In the Vedas she is – by the progenitor Daksha-Prajapati-Kashyapa – the Mother of the Adityas, which is to say, in effect, the mother of the gods (Deva-Matri) themselves, personifications of the ruling principles of the universe. She is perhaps an ancient concept, even an Indus Valley version, of the Great Goddess. The Adityas were personifications of the ruling principles of Vedism and the Universe – inheritance, proper ritual, constancy, the power of words, fate, cosmic law and social law. They include such gods as Mitra, Varuna, Aryaman, Savitri (later the goddess Sarasvati) and an early version of Vishnu. All of these principles are associated with the powers of the Vedic sun god Surya. It must be noted as well that Aditi is also the ultimate destroyer, the consumer of all things in death. As such, she is a precursor of Kali.

What all of these goddesses have in common is their role as 'mothers' of creation – without these beings, nothing that is can be realized. In this sense, Prithvi, Prakriti, Ushas, Vac and Aditi are all the same goddess – prefigurations of the cumulative goddess Devi, whose creative energy activates the potential for existence represented by Dyaus, Purusha, Daksha, Prajapati or Brahma. The various stories of the Vedas are in conflict with each other only in a strict linear and narrative sense. In terms of mytho-logic, they are wholly consistent and serve classical Hinduism as the basis for understandings about the essential unity of the Absolute in its many manifestations and the role of the goddess in her many emanations in relation to it.

The myths of the goddesses of classical Hinduism take form primarily in the *smrti* texts – the Puranas and the epics. They are at once stories of the collective Great Goddess Devi and of the consorts of the important gods, particularly the Hindu Trimurti of Brahma, Vishnu and Shiva: these gods – either individually, in the cases of Vishnu and Shiva, or together as a triad (*trimurti*) – represent the process repeated in each cycle, or *kalpa*, of existence. The process involves the creative passion, the preservation of balance and the necessary ultimate dissolution or destruction. Traditionally, Brahma is the creator, but devotees of Vishnu and Shiva tend to diminish Brahma's role in favour of the dominance of their own great god in all three categories. Preservation, the goodness which maintains balance and order, is, however, generally associated with Vishnu, and dissolution or destruction with Shiva. The worshippers of Vishnu are known as Vaishnavas and those of Shiva as Shaivites.

A third form of devotion, the source of which many would say has effectively replaced Brahma in the Trimurti, is Shaktism, the worship of Shakti, the creative energy Devi. Usually the Shakti takes mythic form as the spouse of Shiva, but all goddesses are emanations of Shakti and can be seen as embodiments of Devi in one or more of her roles, not only as creator, but as preserver and destroyer. The goddesses form a collective Trimurti, which for many Shaktas transcends Vishnu and Shiva and makes Devi the primary embodiment of the unknowable Absolute – the Brahman of the Upanishads – which is neither male nor female, neither there nor here, but everywhere.

As we have seen, the goddess's role in creation is made explicit in the ancient Vedas. Whether Prakriti, Prithvi, Ushas, Vac, Aditi or Sarasvati, she is the necessary element to make the Absolute manifest in creation. In classical Hindu mythology, the goddess continues to play a role in creation. According to the epic poem *Ramayana*, the goddess as Lakshmi arose during the Churning of the Ocean of Milk, when Vishnu – in his form as the Tortoise – dived into the ocean's depths and placed the sacred mountain, which was at risk of sinking beneath the churned waters, on his back, thus establishing a new creation.

The most important emanation of the Hindu goddess in the creation process is Durga. Sometimes seen as the sister of Vishnu and/or the wife of Shiva, Durga is, in a sense, the Shakti of both. Few Hindu deities are more popular than Durga, who is, among her other traits, a terrifying destroyer as well as a force for creation. In connection with her creative aspect, Durga is generally believed to have come into the world as Mahamaya – the great goddess of illusion, that which gives form to the otherwise formless Absolute. As such, she is seen as the power behind creation – Maa Durga, the Mother of Creation. Her purpose was to destroy the representatives of evil that came from the earwax of the sleeping Vishnu and had attacked the creator, Brahma, thereby undermining his work. In short, Durga was the force that challenged the demons who threatened the very basis of creation. According to the Shaktas, Durga, in effect, controlled creation from the very beginning, as the force that fought against evil and awakened the sleeping Vishnu. Durga's most important act of creative destruction was her defeat of the great demon Mahisha, an act which saved creation.

It was known that Mahisha could not be killed by any male. The demon was so powerful that, after attacking the gods, he was able to expel Brahma, Vishnu and Shiva from Heaven. In response, the banished gods created Durga, who, with her eighteen arms (some say ten), rode into Heaven on a lion and announced that she would marry anyone who could overpower her. Mahisha took the bait; he fell in love with the goddess and challenged her to combat. Durga accepted, and when, after a violent battle, Mahisha turned himself into a buffalo demon, she decapitated him with a discus.

This Indian bronze figure from the 16th–18th century depicts the goddess Durga with four arms doing battle against the demon Mahisha in buffalo form, while her lion looks on.

All goddesses are Shakti, in that the gods with whom they are associated can be made manifest only through the goddesses' creative energies. Goddesses are therefore, by definition, creators. This concept is illustrated, for instance, in the popular depiction of Kali, Shiva's wife, dancing upon the passive, reclining form of her husband. In the tantric version of this story, Kali succeeds in arousing Shiva, making him ithyphallic.

Another myth in which the goddess plays a significant role in creation is that of Ganga, the personification of the sacred river Ganges and the mother goddess who descended to earth as did the Sky Maiden of the Native American earth-diver creation myths. In one version of the story, told in the Bhagavata Purana, Ganga comes down to earth on the hair of Shiva, making evident the relationship between the goddess and the god in creation.

Each member of the Hindu Trimurti – Brahma, Vishnu and Shiva – has a wife who embodies Shakti. For Brahma it is Sarasvati, who, over the long period between the Rig Veda and the epics, underwent many transformations. She became Brahma's mate in the Brahmanas, the source of Brahma's creative power, when Brahma was the great creator. In the Puranas, Sarasvati becomes for a while the daughter of Brahma and the cause of the diminishing of his importance when he experienced incestuous lust for her and was punished by the other gods. For a while in the later Puranas, she was the wife of Vishnu until Vishnu gave her away to Brahma; but, for the most part, Sarasvati is important in her own right as a version of Mahadevi, the Great Goddess, in her role as goddess of the creative arts, replacing, in effect, Brahma in the Trimurti.

Vishnu's Shakti wife is almost always Lakshmi. Like Sarasvati, Lakshmi has been an important figure since early Vedic times, when she represented good fortune or prosperity. She and her sister Sri were wives of the ancient progenitor-creator Aditya. One Vedic myth tells how Sri was born of the creator Prajapati as prosperity and how the other gods wanted her gifts and stole them. Later, Sri and Lakshmi were essentially melded into a single figure, Sri Lakshmi. Lakshmi was a significant element in the creation story of the Churning of the Ocean of Milk, arising as she did from the depths of the ocean. By the time of the Puranas and epics, Lakshmi, still representing prosperity and good fortune, is the wife of Vishnu. For Shaktas, Lakshmi is Devi herself and the creative energy that materializes as Vishnu.

The Shakti concept is especially common in relation to Shiva and his spouses, who include, in various contexts, Sati, Parvati (Uma or Gauri), Kali and Durga. In terms of his creative aspect, the most important wife is the goddess Parvati, although all of his wives are, for Shaivites and Shaktas, faces of the universal creative energy that is Devi. Parvati was the daughter of the mountain Himalaya, and was a reincarnation of Shiva's wife Sati, who had committed suicide after her father, Daksha, had snubbed Shiva, thus initiating the practice of sati, in which a Hindu wife is expected to die with her husband. The union of Shiva and Parvati in numerous carvings and in the ubiquitous stone object placed in temples representing the joining of the Shiva *lingam* and the goddess *yoni* are symbolic of fully realized creative energy.

The myths surrounding this union are less theological. In one story, for instance, the lovemaking of Parvati and Shiva was so violent that it shook the earth and the heavens, causing the other gods to complain. Shiva agreed to stop but Parvati did not, and she cursed Mother Earth (Bhumi-Devi) herself, threatening to put an end to the Great Mother's production of children. The relationship between Shiva and Parvati was not always an expression of unity, but it was always related to creation of some sort. The most popular result of their joint creativity is that of the ubiquitously worshipped, immaculately conceived elephant-headed Ganesha, god of wealth and the overcoming of obstacles. There are multiple versions of the story of Ganesha's creation, each of which tell us something of the creativity of the Shiva–Parvati relationship, even when it was dominated by conflict.

The Linga Purana tells of how Shiva created a son, Vigneshwara, from a part of himself that was placed in the womb of Parvati. The Shiva Purana does not deny this version but suggests another, which took place in a more ancient age (kalpa). His immaculate conception here is the more generally accepted myth. Parvati was convinced by her friends that she needed a personal servant, and one day, when Shiva became an unwanted presence while she was taking a bath, she created a protector-son, Vigneshwara, from a bit of something on her skin. When Vigneshwara used violence to prevent Shiva from intruding on Parvati's bath on another occasion, the furious god sent demons and the great Vishnu to try to defeat the upstart. Parvati countered with two angry goddesses who used illusion (*maya*) to protect her son. Vishnu used magic of his own to confuse these goddesses, however, and Shiva succeeded in decapitating Vigneshwara. A furious Parvati then sent a host of vengeful goddeses against the gods, but Shiva deflected defeat by ordering that a new head be found for Parvati's son. The head chosen to replace the old one was that of an elephant, and Vigneshwara became Ganesha, whose name refers to his elephant face. Shiva then accepted him as his son and made him Ganapati, the leader of his demons – the *ganas*.

From the earliest Vedic times and probably earlier in the Indus Valley culture, the goddess in relation to the god – Devi and Deva, Prakriti and Purusha – symbolized cosmic balance: soul and body, the unconscious and the conscious, spirit and matter. The great preserver of the Hindu Trimurti of Brahma, Vishnu and Shiva is Vishnu. It is he who maintains the balance of the universe. According to his worshippers, the Vaishnavas, he is the embodiment of Brahman, the Absolute. When the world falls out of balance, he sends incarnations of himself – avatars – to restore or preserve right actions and duty (dharma). But in the created world Vishnu is inseparable from his Shakti, represented usually by the goddess Lakshmi. His avatars, too, have their Shaktis, avatars of Lakshmi.

According to the Devi Bhagavata Purana, Lakshmi was born from the left side of Vishnu. Once born, she turned herself into two primary aspects of the god: Lakshmi Devi and Radha Devi, Lakshmi as the Shakti-spouse of Vishnu and Radha as the primary Shakti-spouse of Krishna. As goddess of wealth and prosperity, Lakshmi is the perfect Shakti for the preserver god. As noted, Lakshmi takes a creative role in the Churning of the Ocean myth. In that myth, she also takes the form of Padma, the lotus which preserves the gods on its leaves. As the Shakti of the great Vishnu avatar Rama, the hero of the epic the *Ramayana*, she is Sita, born of the ploughed earth. As the daughter of Earth, Bhumi Devi, Sita became the centre of a struggle between her husband Rama and the demon Ravana. Sita was kidnapped by the demon, thus disturbing the world's proper balance, represented by the marriage of Rama and herself, a union which symbolized the universal bala nce of Vishnu-Lakshmi. Only with the defeat of the demon – with the help of the great monkey king Hanuman – and the restoration of Sita to Rama is balance restored. It should be noted here that Hanuman was the son of Mohini, the feminine form taken by Vishnu at the Churning of the Ocean, associating him clearly with Vishnu's role as maintainer of the world in conjunction with the feminine principle. In the *Ramayana*, Sita is depicted, in a patriarchal mode, as the perfect Hindu wife, following her husband loyally regardless of terrible trials and persecution, thus preserving the balance of dharma. The ultimate trial comes when, after her rescue from the demon, she is wrongly accused by the people of a lack of chastity during her long captivity. Eventually, she is rescued from punishment by her mother, who takes her back into herself, Earth.

As the spouse of Vishnu, Lakshmi has many other Shakti-avatars besides Sita. Among the most important are Radha, Draupadi and Rukmini. The balance of the universe was threatened when the evil king Kamsa, inevitably reminding us of King Herod of the biblical story, attempted to prevent the birth of his nephew, Krishna, the most important of the avatars of Vishnu. Krishna was born of Devaki, herself a reincarnation of the Vedic goddess Aditi. Hearing of his birth and fearing his power, Kamsa undertook a massacre of the innocent male babies in his realm. Brought up by foster parents to hide him from Kamsa, Krishna grew in wisdom and spirit. Once when his foster mother scolded him for eating dirt, he opened his mouth for inspection and there his mother saw the whole universe. Krishna was Vishnu, the Absolute. During his years with his foster parents, who were cowherds, Krishna spent much of his time with the cowherd girls, the Gopis. His particular favourite was Radha, whose devotion to Krishna, like the devotion of Sita to Rama, represented the devotion of Krishna's worshippers and, by extension, the worshippers of Vishnu. The lovemaking of Krishna and Radha symbolizes the kind of balance and wholeness represented by the union of Shiva and Parvati in the Shaivite tradition and Vishnu and Lakshmi for the Vaishnavas.

This early 18th-century painting depicts Krishna's devotion to Radha.

Krishna is not always as obviously divine as in these myths, however: in the epic the *Mahabharata*, for instance, he takes a much more mortal form, except in the *Bhagavadgita* section of the epic, where, as the mortal charioteer of the hero Arjuna, he suddenly reveals himself as the incarnation of the Supreme Absolute. As a god on earth, Krishna's Shakti is Radha. As a mortal, he has several wives, of which the most important is Rukmini. The Puranas, however, raise Rukmini to the level of the Lakshmi avatar, tracing her heritage back to the Lakshmi of Churning of the Ocean and even earlier as a granddaughter of Brahma.

Draupadi, like Sita, was one of the Panchakanya, an ideal Hindu woman representing the perfect wife, just as Lakshmi was the perfect wife for Vishnu. Other 'ideal women' included Ahalya, who remained devoted to her husband even when wrongly accused of and punished for being unchaste; Mandodari, the wife of the demon Ravana, who tried to convince her husband not to molest Sita; and Kalindi, the personification of a sacred river and another devoted wife of Krishna. Draupadi is the wife of all five Pandava brothers in the *Mahabharata*. Some say that the Pandavas were the basic atoms (*amsas*) of Vishnu, making their wife an avatar of Lakshmi. When Arjuna, one of the Pandava brothers, announced to his mother Kunti that he had won a great prize, she said he must share any prize with his four brothers.

The prize turned out to be a beautiful princess, Draupadi, and since his mother's declaration could not be withdrawn, Draupadi had to belong to all five brothers. Even when the eldest brother, Yudhisthira, 'lost' her in a famous gambling game with the Pandava enemies, the Kauravas, Draupadi remained faithful and obedient. When the Kauravas, who now owned her, tried to humiliate her by removing her sari, Draupadi was saved, significantly, by the Vishnu avatar Krishna, who made her sari endless in length and, therefore, unremovable. Even after her five sons by the five brothers were killed by the Kauravas and soon thereafter she herself died, Draupadi waited faithfully in heaven for the arrival of her husbands. Draupadi's role, like that of Radha, Sita and Rukmini, was to serve and follow her husband in order to preserve the 'proper' social order of dharma (the cosmic order preserved and maintained by the union of Vishnu and Lakshmi).

In the Panchakanya context, Draupadi, like the other ideal women, represents a stage in the collective Devi's development that suggests something less of a Great Goddess or a Shakti and more like a subservient wife in a highly patriarchal culture. In this context, Parvati (Uma), Shiva's wife, is very different too from the Parvati who denied her husband's entrance to her bath. She is sometimes the dutiful Hindu wife in perfect union with her husband but clearly dominated by him. In the same sense, Sarasvati is portrayed as the perfect wife for Brahma.

In the Trimurti of Brahma, Vishnu and Shiva, Shiva represents destruction or dissolution, a necessary aspect of the process by which the universe is constantly created, preserved and then dissolved before a new creation cycle begins. For Shaivites, whose position is expressed, for instance, in the Shiva Purana, Shiva is the greatest of the gods, combining all three aspects of the Trimurti; Shiva embodies, in short, the Supreme Absolute reality Brahman. Shiva's roots are almost certainly in the pre-Vedic Harrapan culture, where seals indicate a three-headed god sat cross-legged, in a position that some scholars suggest represents his role as the ultimate yogi. A further development of the deity who would become Shiva is the Rudra of the Vedas, a warrior storm god who is sometimes, in fact, referred to as Shiva ('the Auspicious One'). In several versions of his story he is created as an expression of Brahma's anger. In the tantric tradition, one in which yoga is a significant element and in which the masculine and feminine are united in the quest for transcendence (moksha), Shiva is sometimes the terrifying Bhairava, who combines with the goddess as Bhairavi and who is, in effect, the terrifying Kali. As the Lord of the Dance, Shiva embodies the process of existence itself. As a dancer and as a destroyer, his counterpart, his energizing force, is Kali, the destroyer goddess who dances on his body. Kali is, of course, an aspect of Devi, as are the other aspects of Shiva's Shakti: Durga and Parvati (Uma). Kali is the black goddess, the dark side of the Shakti. She is Parvati's anger and the destructive side of Durga's power: Durga and Kali are often the same being. For some, especially tantrists and Shaktas, Kali is the Absolute Brahman.

Whatever the interpretation, Kali is said to be the voracious consumer of time (*kala*), which brings into reality the Absolute timelessness that, for Shaivites, is Shiva. Dancing on Shiva, her four arms raised, with one arm holding a human skull, another a bent sword and her mouth dripping blood, her tongue protruding and her hair wild, she is garlanded with human skulls: in the most obvious sense, Kali, with her rosary of skulls, represents the necessity of death. Her sword is said to be 'divine knowledge' and the skull in her left hand is said to be the human self-centred consciousness which knowledge must eliminate. As pointed out earlier in connection with her ecstatic dance on the inert body of Shiva, Kali is the cosmic energy without which Shiva is merely dead matter. There is a sexual aspect to Kali's power represented by this image; in the tantric tradition she stands over the ithyphallic Shiva, not as the subservient ideal Hindu woman, but as a sexually liberated breaker of traditional female boundaries.

It is generally thought that Kali's origins are pre-Vedic. The Matsya Purana says she was born on Mount Kalinjara in northeast India. A possible precursor goddess is the dark-skinned demon Nirrti of the Vedic Taittiriya Brahmana, a personification of decay and annihilation, who, like the Greek Furies, chases down sinners. In the Kathaka Grhya Sutra, Kali is mentioned, and in the Mundaka Upanishad she is one of the tongues of the Vedic fire god Agni. As a tongue of the fire god, Kali here is clearly associated with sacrifice: in terms of the cosmos and the individual life, existence depends not only on creation and preservation but also on destruction, the

This *c.* 17th-century Indian wooden sculpture (with traces of paint) depicts the fearsome face of the goddess Kali.

consumption enacted in the sacrificial fire. Later Kali – and Shiva – will be depicted dancing in the ashes of cremation grounds, signifying this sacrifice and consumption, Kali's blackness representing death and perhaps the earth to which the dead return as ash.

In the *Mahabharata*, in which Kali is a personification of death in this epic's great war, Devi in her form as Gauri refuses a king's proposal of marriage and springs from her own head as Kali to attack the king when he does not accept the refusal. In the tale's war, it is Kali who takes the dead warriors back to herself. She appears as Kaalratri (Black Night) to the Pandavas in a dream on the battlefield, like the Greek deities who join the Trojan War battles in Homer's *Iliad*. Most of Kali's myths are told in the Puranas, particularly in the Shakta texts, the Devi Mahatmya, part of a Purana attributed to the sage Markandeya, and in the Devi Bhagavatam, or Devi Purana. A tantric version of Kali appears as Kamakhya or Mahamaya (meaning desire and illusion, respectively) in the Kalika Purana. In these Puranas, Devi as Kali is the face of Brahman. She exists as Shakti on her own, not as the Shakti of a male god, and perhaps has her roots in the ancient pre-Vedic Great Goddess.

As we have already discussed, Kali is often associated with Durga, the ferocious manifestation of Devi as the slayer of the monstrous Mahisha at the time of creation. In one myth, Kali sprang from Durga's forehead, as Devi's anger, to kill Mahisha. Another story has Kali emerging from Durga's head as Chamunda – another form of the destroying goddess – to kill two demons. In this case Kali is, in effect, one of the Sapta-Matrikas, the 'Seven Mothers'. The Matrikas personified the Shakti power of various gods: Brahmani emerged from Brahma, Vaishnavi from Vishnu, Mahashaveri from Shiva, Indrani from Indra, Kaumari from Skanda (a war god), Varahi from the Vishnu boar avatar and Chamunda from Devi, becoming Kali.

There are conflicting stories about the creation of the Matrikas and their nature. In one version, they are created by Shiva to help him defeat the demon Andhaka, who attempted to kidnap Parvati. When Shiva wounded the demon with his arrow, thousands of other Andukas sprang from the blood. The Matrikas had the ability to drink the demon blood before it reached the ground, and so defeated the demons, but also absorbed their evil, which they used against the gods until they were expelled by Shiva.

Another myth describes how Devi as Durga created the Matrikas from her own being. In this myth, the Mothers assist Durga in her fight against demons. One of the Matrikas was Kali – also called Chamunda here – who sucked all of the demon blood. Later, Durga took the Matrikas back into herself as warlike aspects of her collective nature. For some, these tales of Kali and the demons are allegories of a perceived struggle between the ancient pre-Vedic Great Goddess and the patriarchal culture that threatened her.

Kali's blood-drinking has many mythic aspects. In one story she dances wildly, drunk on the blood of her victims, becoming a threat to the universe itself, which echoes the Egyptian goddess Sekhmet, whose bloodthirsty punishment of the world threatens its existence, causing the high god to intervene. In this case it is Shiva himself who intervenes by lying down in front of the goddess. When she steps on him, Shiva is able to restrain her and thus save the universe. Another version of this theme is found in a tale of Shiva as an infant restraining Kali. Once again, Kali has defeated her enemies and is drunk on their blood, and so Shiva comes to the battleground as a crying infant, appealing to Kali's maternal sympathy and calming her destructive wrath. She picks up the child and breastfeeds him. In this act we find an image of Kali in her form as the mother goddess, Kali Maa.

Although two of Kali's four hands hold instruments of violence, the other two are raised in signs of greeting and blessing. The Mother greets and blesses us, nurturing us even as she kills and drinks blood. In fact, in Kali's most recent incarnation as Kali Maa, she is all things, all aspects of the process symbolized by the Hindu Trimurti. She is the cosmic energy – the Shakti – from which the universe is born. Her dance, like Shiva's, preserves and maintains life itself, and her seemingly brutal connection with blood and death can also suggest a loving absorption of the world back into herself at the end of a life or the end of an age. In short, as Mother Earth, everything that emerges from her is also preserved by her and ultimately is returned to her.

Who then is this dark goddess of contradictions? She is a face of Devi, who, like Brahman, has no face, no myths, except in relation

This early 19th-century British lithograph of original drawings of traditional Indian sculptures of Kali shows some of the most important guises of the goddess.

to the faces she wears. Kali is Durga the demon-slayer, Shakti the cosmic energy of Shiva, who dances with him in the cremation fields. But she is also the same goddess who takes the loving wifely forms of Sarasvati, Lakshmi and Parvati. And she is the ancient Prakriti (Matter) linked to Purusha (Soul); most of all, she is Prithvi – the Mother who, in order to sustain life, must take on the role of the blessed if painful destroyer, Death herself.

The goddess Durga killing the buffalo demon (Mahishasura Mardini),
from the Pala period, 12th century, Bangladesh or India.

II

The Religious Conversion of the Near Eastern Goddess

Genesis

The name Iran comes from Aryanam, an ancient, unattested Indo-European term which appears in Sanskrit as *arya* and in Avestan as *airya*, and which is known in similar forms in Greek and Latin. From this root we get the word 'Aryan', which refers to the wide range of Iranian influence not limited to the political borders of either ancient or modern Iran. Persia, on the other hand, comes from Parsa, the name of a single province of ancient Iran. That same region is now known as Fars, and the language of modern Iran is Farsi, just as the name of the ancient language is commonly known as Persian. 'Iran' is now the preferred term because it is broader and more fully encompassing, while Persia is a narrower and less inclusive appellation.

The name Persia captured the classical imagination for good reason, however: Parsa, in the southwest of Iran, was an extraordinarily important region, spawning two of the great dynasties of that empire, the Achaemenid and the Sassanian, which ruled from the sixth to the fourth centuries BCE and the third to the seventh centuries CE, respectively. The name Persia, then, was indelibly linked in the minds of the Greeks with the ruling classes and excesses of their mighty enemies to the east. Parsa has been known as Fars since the assimilation of the Persian Empire into the larger Islamic Caliphate, for the practical reason that Arabic has no letter 'p'. Thus, although it is technically correct to refer to Iran, there are historically significant reasons why that land was commonly known as Persia in western Europe until fairly recently.

This ram head figure dates from 600–300 BCE and hails from western Iran.

The history of Iran is exceedingly long and complex, but in brief, the Achaemenid dynasty ruled what has long been called the Persian Empire from the mid-sixth century to the late fourth century BCE. The Achaemenids reached their peak under Darius I, who ruled a broad swathe stretching from the eastern Mediterranean (well into Greece and coastal North Africa) all the way east into India, and reaching north along the coasts of the Black, Caspian and Aral Seas. The Iranian expansion ended by the first third of the fifth century BCE with unsuccessful attempts to annex the Greek city-states into the Persian Empire, and in 330 BCE the Iranian humiliation was completed by the conquest of Alexander the Great, remembered ever after in eastern lore as the mighty monarch Iskandar. The next 200 years saw the rise of a Helleno-Persian state, founded by a follower of Alexander and known as the Seleucid Empire, which absorbed most of the Iranian region. The Parthian Empire, a pan-Iranian state under the Arsacid dynasty, rose to power around 247 BCE, and waned around 220 CE. From 224 CE until the mid-seventh century, the Zoroastrian-dominated Sassanid dynasty held sway. The seventh-century onslaught of the Arabs brought an end to the Sassanians, bringing an Islamic caliphate which wrought significant and abiding transformations upon Iranian language and culture.

Zoroaster, as we generally call him after the fashion of the Greeks, or Zarathustra, as he originally was known to the ancient Iranians, founded a dualist religion about a thousand years before the birth of Christ, and Zoroastrianism was the dominant faith throughout much of the Near East and western Asia until the time of the conversion of that region to Islam some seven centuries after Christ. Zoroaster taught that the universe was a battleground between Good and Evil, the powers of which were more or less equal. The forces of Good were led by Ahura Mazda, while those of Evil followed Ahriman. Zoroaster, who was exceedingly well versed in the ancient religion he came to transform, taught his followers to view the myths of the ancient Iranians through a new lens, one which emphasized one's personal choices and actions in the constant battle between cosmic forces. According to Zoroastrianism, fire is the ultimate agent of purification, although it is incorrect to designate the followers of Zoroaster as fire-worshippers, a misconception which they find demeaning and offensive. After the advent of Islam, Zoroastrianism was tolerated throughout the Muslim world as a religion of the book, rather like Christianity and Judaism. In reality, however, most people in the region converted to the new religion within a few generations. Today Zoroastrianism is still practised by a number of believers in Iran, by the Parsee community in India and in various diaspora communities throughout the world. The most lasting impact of Zoroastrianism in Western religion, mythology and philosophy was the dualism preached by Mani, which drew upon the foundational beliefs of that ancient faith of Zoroaster in order to reinterpret the teachings of Christ. Mani himself died a martyr for his faith in the late third century; Manichaeism, meanwhile, was declared heretical by the Roman Catholic Church, as were later dualist sects which perhaps owed a doctrinal debt to Mani, such as the Cathars.

Avestan, the sacred language of the Zoroastrians, is derived from the eastern branch of the Iranian language tree. For many generations, the sacred texts of the Avesta, the Zoroastrian collection of sacred scripture, were passed down verbatim from one generation of priests to the next, and absolute fidelity to the precise language of the original version was sacrosanct, even if the meaning itself might have been unclear. Thus the transmission of the Avesta was extraordinarily conservative, and the modern text represents a strong link to the ancient oral traditions from whence it sprang. The Avesta was probably first written down in the first or second century CE, and a now-lost complete version might have been recorded by the sixth century or so. The Avesta as we know it today only dates back some 600–700 years, however, and merely represents a small percentage, perhaps one-quarter, of the original text, mostly that concerned with religious rituals.

The Avesta is divided into several main parts: the Gathas are the seventeen hymns of Zoroaster, and they themselves comprise part of the larger Yasna. Linguistic evidence provides compelling connections between these hymns and those of the ancient, devotional Rig Veda, and which thus belong to the era of the Indo-Iranian people before they moved into the lands which have since borne their names. The Khordeh Avesta, or 'Little Avesta', is another section, as is the Vendidad or Videvdat, the 'Law against the Demons', and the Visperad. Of special note are the Yasht and the Yasna, the latter of which includes the prayers and chants necessary to the eponymous Zoroastrian ritual.

The 24 hymns of the Yasht, moreover, are of particular interest to students of ancient mythology, as they evoke early gods and spirits, and thus contain a great deal of pre-Zoroastrian pagan material; many of the heroic episodes of the Yasht are also compiled in the great Iranian epic the *Shahnameh*, or 'Book of Kings', completed by the poet Ferdowsi in around 1010 CE. Ferdowsi's work is the most fully developed and best known of a school of Islamic antiquarians who were fascinated by and recorded the ancient tales of the Iranians. The first European translation of the Avesta, into French, was not completed until the late eighteenth century and was highly criticized; the bible of the Zoroastrians was not translated into English until about a century later.

'Iranian' properly refers to a great branch of the Indo-European language family; 'Persian' is a smaller subgroup within Iranian. Persian was and continues to be a widely spoken language: in addition to Farsi, the primary language of modern Iran, a version of this tongue called Tajik is the official language of Tajikistan, as well as being the mother tongue of a great many people in southern Uzbekistan and western Afghanistan. Known there as Dari, Persian is in fact the most widespread language in Afghanistan; furthermore, the official tongue of that country, Pashto, is also a cousin from the Iranian family. It is vital to keep in mind that this family of languages, although transformed by contact with the Arabic language and Islamic culture, is related to most European languages, and its links to ancient Greek and Latin are often compelling. Most important of all, the wellspring of the Iranian languages was also that of Sanskrit, the classical language of the Indian subcontinent. These linguistic relationships are not incidental because these ancient cultures also shared common mythological ancestors, and thus many names and myths of each have much to teach us about the others. That said, it is undeniable that Iranian languages and letters underwent a sea-change after the conversion to Islam.

First of all, the imposition of Arabic script had a discernable phonetic impact upon Persian, illustrated, for example, by the difference between Persian or Parsee and Farsi: Persian is written with Arabic script, and as noted, Arabic has no letter 'p'. In addition, both sacred and secular Arabic loanwords flooded the language after the conquest. What is often called New Persian had risen to prominence as the second great literary language of the Islamic world by the time of Ferdowsi, and this language has, moreover, remained fairly stable; thus, a modern speaker of Farsi has little trouble reading the medieval poet's *Shahnameh*. Most importantly, just as the Persian language was changed through its contact with Arabic, mythology became similarly transformed, but not destroyed, through its transmission via Islamic authors. Firmly Islamic though it may be, Iran has a long tradition of rightful pride in its ancient roots and glories, and the face of the ancient Iranian goddess, although refracted through an Islamic lens, is still discernible through the later texts which contain traces of her earliest manifestations.

Faces of the Goddess

The nurturing and beneficent figure of the Cosmic Cow looms significantly around the edges of Iranian mythology. According to Zoroastrian creation stories, in the beginning there was the Proto-Man and the

Ur-Cow, who lived together peacefully until they were destroyed by the powers of darkness; all creation was subsequently brought into being by utilizing the matter from the corpses of these great, primal beings. In this regard, Iranian creation myth bears striking parallels to its distant Norse cousin (discussed further in Chapter Four); given that they descend at least in some measure from a shared Indo-European mythological heritage, this may perhaps be less surprising than it might at first seem. In Scandinavian mythology, the Cosmic Cow Audhumla suckles the original giant Ymir, from whose body all the world is wrought; this bovine, life-force goddess literally laps the first man into existence with her tongue, forming him from a great primordial salt-lick. Moreover, the Cosmic Cow is not the only representation of the Great Goddess apparent in Iranian creation mythology. While we learn from the *Bundahishn* of Zoroastrian tradition that Ahura Mazda embodies both the aspects of the mother goddess and those of the father god, nurturing creation within his own form as a mother would a child, the great Earth Goddess Spendarmad preserves and protects the seed of Gayomart inside the earth, and after its purification it is fertilized within her and she bears its fruit, two humans born of rhubarb plants from whom the race is sprung. Evil, like Good, is androgynous in Zoroastrian tradition, and much as Ahura Mazda could be both father and mother of creation, some sources suggest that the Evil One begat his demon progeny by impregnating himself in his own anus.

The female embodiment of Evil is Jeh, the Great Whore, the ultimate cause of the corruption and downfall of the First Man, who as the champion of Good promised to wreak havoc with the plans of Ahriman, Lord of Evil. When Ahriman realized that the First Man was his enemy, he fell into a stupor of despair that lasted 3,000 years. Each of his vile minions took it in turn to whisper into the ear of their lord a plot to despoil the First Man, but Ahriman remained unconscious until Jeh promised to corrupt the Righteous Man. The Evil One then awoke, and in his joy he kissed his concubine upon her forehead, at which she began to menstruate, an unclean mark which she subsequently passed down to all women. Sometimes described as the consort of the Evil One, Jeh is thus in clear opposition to Spendarmad, the consort of the Good One. The name Jeh is cognate with Jahi, which originally denoted 'woman' in Avestan, but which came to be associated with fallen or flawed women, and thus with sexual incontinence specifically. Jeh, then, is the name used most notably in the *Bundahishn* to name the Great Whore who caused the downfall of the Righteous Man in the earliest times, while Jahi is the more conceptual figure of 'Debauchery' and is often counted as one of the evil figures in the ranks of the demonic abstractions.

As the Great Mother brings life into being, so does she stand at the border to death, and it is she who acts as judge and guide to the departed. The Chinvat Bridge acts as the passage between the land of the living and the realm of the dead, where each wandering soul meets a figure who determines how that soul's life shall be judged and where it shall abide ever after. In a duality which reflects certain faces of the Three Goddesses and the maiden and crone of Celtic tradition, as well as some aspects of Scandinavian mythology, the actions of one's life determine whether one is met at the bridge to the next world by a beautiful, sweetly perfumed maiden or a horrific, foul-smelling hag; while the former leads to peace in paradise, the latter is a harbinger of perdition and torment. Again, the terrible beauty of the goddess is manifested at the very moment of death.

According to the doctrines revealed by Zoroaster, the cosmic forces of Good and Evil – or what we might alternatively conceive as right and wrong religion or belief – are in constant and nearly evenly matched struggle. Zoroaster described a duality between *asha* (*aša*), 'truth', and *druj* (*drug*), 'lie', which has truly ancient roots, as reflected in the Vedic Indian concepts of *rta* and *druh*, and which extends into modern languages and conceptions, as in the German word for 'deception', *Trug*. Zoroaster, however, went a step further, personifying the individual attributes of truthfulness and deceit into the archetypal spirits, or the Great Angels Spenta Mainyu, 'Holy Spirit', and Angra Mainyu, 'Maleficent Spirit'. The Avestan term *spenta* is related to an ancient Sanskrit term for 'strong', *isira*, as well as to the Greek *hieros*, or 'holy', and has exact parallels in the Lithuanian and Old Church Slavonic words for 'holy', *sventas* and *svetu*, respectively. The figure of Spenta Mainyu itself faded over time in Zoroastrian belief, and was later replaced by a set of personifications of various attributes of beneficence known as the Amesha Spentas, or 'Immortal Holy Ones', the seven sons and daughters – a set of archangels in the Zoroastrian monotheistic firmament – of Ahura Mazda, the Zoroastrian supreme being and force for good. Some of these figures were male and some female, and some of the feminine spirits offer telling glimpses of aspects of the ancient Iranian goddess.

Armaiti, 'faithful devotion and right-thinking', is one such Amesha Spenta; these archangels – or immortal sons and daughters of God – are the individual facets of the Divine Being, representing the protective forces which watch over the seven sub-creations that in Zoroastrian thought comprise the totality of Divine Creation. Each of these forces both guards and may be symbolized by a particular element of creation. Armaiti protects the earth, and is represented by the consecrated site of her ritual. Like all the Amesha Spentas, Armaiti has her gilded high seat in the abode of the righteous, known to later Zoroastrian belief as the House of Song. Seated to the left of Ahura Mazda, Armaiti is the personification of the proper and thoughtful performance of religious ritual and spiritual discipline, and therefore to manifest the great faith-fulness of the Prophet of Zoroastrianism, Armaiti is believed to have deigned to have granted Zoroaster a vision of herself in bodily form. Armaiti rejoices in righteousness and is dismayed by deceit, treachery and disrespect. Her great enemies include Taromaiti and Pairimaiti, spirits of evil intent, arrogance and wrong-headedness. Her identity as a guardian of the earth also designated her as a patroness of cattle, animal husbandry and agriculture, and she is the spirit which provides good pasturage. Armaiti's ancient roots as one of the great faces of the goddess in the Indo-Iranian tradition is reflected by the fact that a cognate form, Aramati, appears in the Indian Rig Veda, wherein she is designated Gna Devi, or 'Woman Goddess'. The later form of Armaiti's name, Spendarmad, conflates her identity as a Spenta, 'holy spirit', with her characteristic Armaiti, or 'sacred devotion'. Armaiti has long been identified as a later Zoroastrian reflection of one face of the ancient Iranian goddess Anahita.

Haurvatat and Ameretat, 'Integrity' and 'Immortality', are the dual faces of the Goddess of Eternal Salvation in Iranian mythology. Both words are feminine in gender in Avestan, and certainly were female in their earliest scriptural references. That the former is the Iranian face of an ancient figure is illustrated by the fact that her name is related to the Indian term *sarvatat* and the Greek *holotes*, both of

This seal has been traced to 4th- or 5th-century BCE Iran but seems to have been acquired in a bazaar in Kabul, Afghanistan, in the early to mid-19th century CE. It displays the Iranian goddess Anahita with a lion.

which might be rendered as 'wholeness'. Likewise, the latter name is cognate with the Sanskrit *amrtatvam* and the Greek *ambrosia*, both of which connote immortality. These two goddesses are always named together, and they represent the totality of eternal life and everlasting bliss in their combination of moral wholeness of spirit and deathlessness. They bring to mind and are most likely derived from the ancient Indo-European mythological concept of the 'divine twins', and many parallels may be drawn with the male Ashvins, twins of Hindu mythology, who among other attributes were associated with the healing properties of waters and plants.

The other attributes of Haurvatat and Ameretat illustrate the ancient role of the goddess as giver of life: they are associated with life-giving waters and burgeoning vegetation, with the cattle of the fields and with the wealth such livestock represent. Therefore, these twin goddesses embody sources of life-giving force associated with rigorous discipline, a discipline understood to be both physical and moral. Thus in the persons of Haurvatat and Ameretat, the ancient role of fecundity ever associated with the goddess is melded with a moral righteousness and spiritual steadfastness, which we might see as an outgrowth of later stable, settled agricultural civilizations. The eternal foes of Haurvatat and Ameretat are traditionally Hunger and Thirst, and considering the moral and spiritual attributes of these goddesses, one suspects that metaphorical moral and spiritual lack is reflected in this regard, in addition to literal physical dearth. Echoes of these goddesses are discerned in the myths and folktales of peoples who were influenced by the Iranians, and thus appear in both Jewish and Arabic texts. In the Qur'an, for example, the angels Harut and Marut pursue a maiden who is ultimately fixed in the firmament as the planet Venus, called Zohra. Other versions of the same tale use the Iranian name for Venus, Anahid, which is clearly derived from the name of the goddess Anahita; this goddess is associated with the planet Venus in Iranian cosmology. The direct Iranian mythic sources for such episodes are lost, but the many tales about the very male Indian divine twins may help us to provide some context for the fragments about their Iranian cousins which remain, even as they also call into question any easy assumptions about gender roles and sexuality regarding the mythic sources and narrative development of these divinities.

In addition to the Amesha Spentas, the Yazatas, or Worshipful Ones, inhabit the heavenly sphere, third in rank behind Ahura Mazda and the Amesha Spentas. The Yazatas are generally the embodiment of ideals or the watchful spirits associated with celestial bodies. There are, therefore, no set number of Yazatas, although the best known are those most closely associated with days of the Zoroastrian calendar, or those which have Yashts or hymns dedicated to them. Although the Yazatas might be thought to have descended from ancient deities, they are not properly compared to gods in contemporary Zoroastrianism, which should be understood as monotheistic. Rather, in modern Zoroastrianism it is probably more appropriate to consider the Yazatas to be almost akin to Catholic saints or angels. Rather like saints, the Worshipful Ones act as intermediaries, and may be beseeched to intercede with Ahura Mazda on behalf of petitioners.

Ardvi Sura Anahita, perhaps best rendered 'Powerful, Pure, Wetness', is one of the greatest of the Yazatas; her name is a combination of features encapsulated by Old Persian adjectives: Ardvi and Sura are relatively commonplace terms, while Anahita, unknown as a word distinct from the goddess of that name, has been interpreted in the context of the worship of the goddess and in that of comparative mythology. She has been linked with the Roman Juno, as well as with the Slavic watered earth goddess Mati Syra Zemlya, 'Moist Mother Earth'. Anahita is the source of life-giving water; by extension, she is the source of all life, and primary cleanser of seed, womb and milk. Anahita's springs are formed by the thousand lakes within the vast cosmic ocean Vourukasha beyond the mountain Alburz. Yasht Five of the Avesta, the Aban Yasht, is dedicated to She of the Undefiled Waters. When Zoroaster enquires as to the proper form of her worship, the goddess replies that it is fitting to sacrifice to her throughout the period between sunrise and sunset by quaffing her sacred beverage.

The chariot of the Goddess of Undefiled Waters is pulled by four steeds, Wind, Rain, Cloud and Sleet. Anahita's association with her great celestial chariot is not an incidental one: in addition to her nature as the embodiment of powerful, unpolluted waters, through her identity as bringer of life, her role as patroness of herds and crops, and her function as the ultimate source of all waters and fertility, Anahita is also identified as a giver of temporal gifts, most especially chariots and horses. This equine association is a common one in Indo-European goddesses, especially those who patronize warriors; the Celtic Epona is perhaps the most obvious example of this type of deity. It is, moreover, but a short step from the giving of steeds for the stable to the granting of victory on the battlefield. She Who is the Fount of All Life is obviously to be seen as a rational choice for pragmatic petitioners who seek the ultimate protector of such life, and thus warriors might naturally pray to such a goddess, in the first place for protection in battle, but also by logical extension for victory in war. Thus we see in the figure of the Iranian Anahita a perfect example of the terrible beauty of the ancient Indo-European goddess of old, whose radiant visage blesses both life-giving sources of vitality and procreation, and life-taking acts of carnage and war.

Yasht Five provides an extraordinarily detailed portrait of Anahita, and we are told that she was well-born of the most noble of races, bedecked in a golden mantel and with a golden crown upon her head, a circlet adorned with eight rays and a hundred stars. To grace her lovely visage, the goddess wears square earrings of gold, as well as a golden necklace. At all times, She of the Undefiled Waters bears the baresma (or barsom, a bouquet of hallowed sticks) in her hand. The rich descriptions of the physical appearance of Anahita lead us to believe that statuary played a role in her rituals, and the historical record bears out this assumption: indeed, graven images of

Anahita seem to have been commonplace before the conversion to Islam. Anahita's derivation from an ancient fertility goddess and her continued embodiment of the powers of life and fertility is suggested in many ways. She was the object of veneration and gratitude by followers throughout a broad swathe of the ancient world, far beyond the borders of Iran, and the Greek historian Berossus records that statues of Anahita were raised and worshipped in centres as varied as Armenia, Babylon and Damascus. A Roman historian tells a more scurrilous tale which, true or not, clearly indicates how closely the goddess was associated with fecundity, sexuality and procreation: according to Strabo, the rites of Anahita in Anatolia demanded that the daughters of the nobility practise ritual prostitution in her temples before they were sanctified in matrimony. Other sources, however, indicate that Anahita was served by virgin votaries instead, and it is important to note that prohibition against prostitution is commonplace in the holy scriptures of Zoroastrianism.

Warriors, heroes and villains all regularly pray and make sacrifices to Anahita for victory and life; offering sacrifice to Anahita sometimes serves to underscore the relationships between ancient, mythic Iranian and Zoroastrian traditions and texts, and the much later antiquarian literary texts of Islamic Iran, most notably the *Shahnameh* – the very title of which, 'Book of Kings', emphasizes the goal of encapsulating the tales and histories of the ancient monarchies of Iran. A classic case in point involves Azhi Dahaka, perhaps best translated as 'Snake Fiend' or 'Dragon Demon', and rendered *azhdaha* in modern Farsi. A triple-headed monster with an insatiable appetite for human flesh, Azhi Dahaka is described in detail in Yasht Nine of the Avesta. In the Aban Yasht, moreover, we learn that the three-headed Dragon Devil sacrificed one hundred stallions, one thousand oxen and ten thousand lambs, beseeching the beneficent goddess to allow him to empty the seven lands of the earth of all men. Azhi Dahaka is finally imprisoned in the bowels of Mount Damavand by Thraetona, the mighty hero who will re-emerge in the *Shahnameh* as Feridun, where he will again be pitted against the serpent demon, in this context known as the evil King Zohak. On the other hand, Haoshanha, first king of the Paradata dynasty, implores Anahita in the Aban Yasht for assistance in his quest to overpower the demons and forces of darkness. Haoshanha reappears in the *Shahnameh* as Hushang of the Pishdadian dynasty. The ancient Avestan Anahita is, in a sense, literally converted to a new, Islamic form when Fatima, daughter of the Prophet, takes on the epithet of the Powerful Pure One; Islamic women were strongly encouraged to take Fatima as a role model, especially in terms of her demure obedience, maternal love and moral rectitude. That in some measure Fatima appropriated ancient aspects of Anahita, including her association as a mother goddess with life-giving force and especially with purity, is emphasized by the fact that Fatima became, over time, described as Zohar, the 'radiant' one, a designation formerly reserved for Anahita.

The Pairaka of the Avesta transform in the Iranian epic tradition into the Peri, or Pari in modern Farsi; both the word and the concept seem related to the 'fairy' of the British Isles. The Pairaka, we are told, are chiefly creatures of the night, although they may appear in daylight, and these shape-shifting witches could appear in forms as varied as a shooting star or a rummaging rodent. Pairaka could appear bewitchingly beautiful to beguile the unwary, and in Persian literature of the Middle Ages to have a Peri-like appearance meant to have unsurpassable beauty. In the ancient texts we learn that Mithra was one of the chief enemies of the Pairaka and the demonic Divs. Although in later texts the Peris are somewhat morally ambivalent and not necessarily evil, traditionally, the Pairaka were unambiguously evil and clearly associated with the forces of darkness. To cite just one example, when the foul, dragon-shouldered King Zohak raised an army to protect himself against the hero Feridun in the *Shahnameh*, the evil tyrant specifically enlisted Peri and demons in addition to men. This ancient association of the Pairaka with shape-shifting dark magic, in the context of the later understanding of the superhuman beauty of the Peri, recalls the terrible beauty of the fairies of the Celtic tradition and even the Valkyries of Scandinavian myth. In each case, feminine beauty and sexual allure are combined with dangerous and threatening power over life and death in a potent mythic cocktail.

Nausch is a maleficent female spirit who reigned supreme over the demons, or Divs. *Divs* is a word closely related to the Latin *deus*, which derives from the ancient term *daeva*, which could mean either a true god or a false deity. In the most fully developed Zoroastrian narratives, Nausch appears in the guise of a speckled fly, and her home is said to be in the far North. In the Iranian tradition, the North is the fount-spring and realm of all evil; this is an association with clear resonances to the Scandinavian and classical traditions, in which the world of the dead is found in the North. Nausch is, perhaps, to be compared to Hel, the ruler of the dead in the Norse tradition: she also lives to the North and in the realm below. She is of variegated appearance, and her half-decaying body and empire of corpses surely may be associated with flies. Nausch may be classed with those evil spirits generically known as *druj*.

Like the Divs and the earliest forms of the untrustworthy Pairaka, the *druj* are a class of evil beings; the modern Farsi word for 'lie' is *durugh*, which is related to the German noun *Trug* for 'deception' or 'a swindle', as well as to the verb *trügen*, which means 'to deceive'. Indeed, in ancient Iranian tradition *druj*, 'falsehood', is in opposition with *asha*, 'truth', both as a philosophical concept and in terms of generic categories of mythic cosmic beings. As a study of the Amesha Spentas makes clear, comparative analysis of early Indo-European mythology illustrates the very ancient roots of this duality, which mirrors that in the Indian Vedic tradition, in which *druj* and *rta* provide a similar dichotomy. The *druj* are, then, most properly understood as the evil twins or negative photographical images of the Immortal Holy Ones, at least in theory. They in any case must be understood to represent the forces of Evil in constant and nearly evenly matched conflict with those of Good in the Zoroastrian universe. In ancient Iranian ritual, moreover, a prayer against the moral malaise represented by Drauga, the Great 'Lie', was typical, and was echoed in other Indo-European traditions.

Nasu is an ancient figure which exemplifies how the goddess so often manifests a terrible beauty, ever pairing the wonder of life force and fecundity with concomitant terror, destruction and decay. The name comes from a word denoting 'dead flesh', and the term is, in fact, related to the Greek word *nekus*, 'dead body'. An evocative figure in the ancient collection of Iranian demigods and demons, because of her foundational role at the end of every life as the primal force which causes dead matter to decay, Nasu continues to exert a powerful hold on Zoroastrian believers today. Indeed, the ancient belief in Nasu still permeates modern Zoroastrian funeral rites, as this demoness of destruction and decay is believed to possess the bodies of the dead. During funeral rituals, therefore, the officiates and mourners do not touch the corpse, which is handled only by Nasar-salas, or 'corpse-bearers', who occupy an untouchable niche in Zoroastrian society. Unlike those oppressed by the caste system in India, however, Nasar-salas may re-enter society after ending their occupation and undergoing a nine-day cleansing rite known as *bareshnum*.

Death is a form of victory of the powers of Evil over those of Good, and thus Zoroastrian funeral rites are largely concerned with purification of the defilement embodied by Nasu. The Nasar-salas use nails to define a tangible border demarking the area of pollution caused by the corpse; a dog is employed to perform the *sagdid* ritual, whereby the demonic forces are kept at bay. The holier the deceased, the greater the victory of the powers of Evil, and hence the greater the opportunity for spiritual pollution. Funerals must take place during the day, when evil forces are least powerful, and ideally upon the day of death itself. If the funeral must be postponed overnight, officiants and mourners stand vigil, but never a solitary vigil, as Nasu and her demonic sisters wax too strong during the hours of darkness; a dog will return to perform additional *sagdid* rituals at prescribed points throughout the night.

Another demon associated with death and decay is Asto-Vidatu, roughly rendered as 'Body-Rot'. Asto-Vidatu is perhaps of most interest in terms of comparative mythology, as she is another figure that emphasizes reflections of terrible beauty between Indo-European traditions across continents and millennia. Most specifically, like Nasu, Asto-Vidatu bears some relationship to Lua Mater, 'Mother of Corruption', the battle goddess in whose name successful Roman soldiers sacrificed the plundered arms and armour of their vanquished foes. The Indian cousin of these goddesses of destruction and decay is the Vedic Nirrti, the 'Decomposer', whose name is drawn from the terms *nirr-* and *rta-*, 'decompose' and 'order', respectively. Nirrti was a demonic force to be avoided or to be set upon one's enemies; thus her name is often evoked as a curse upon others or in supplications to other deities for protection against the evil forces of decay represented by this goddess. Moreover, there are interesting legal similarities which further emphasize the mythic connections concerning destruction and decay between ancient Iran and ancient Rome, especially in terms of fines and penalties regarding the breaching of prohibitions concerning decomposing bodies. Even the Latin term for the ritual cleansing of those involved in funeral rituals, *denicales feriae*, draws upon the root *nec-*, from *nex*, 'dead material', which is linguistically linked to *nasu*.

The epic tales of Iranian heroes often underscore the function and powers of the goddess within this mythology. For example, the story of Feridun in the *Shahnameh* contains an explicit reference to a river crossing which seems both to draw upon and to develop the function of Anahita as the Great Goddess associated with the Pure Undefiled Waters, she who in ancient Iranian tradition also acts as the patroness of military victory to those who properly seek her aid. The terrible beauty of Anahita is thus revealed: she is both goddess of life-giving waters and dispenser of death-dealing victory in battle. In this episode, Anahita is evident in the form of the Arvand River, which stands literally as a barrier in Feridun's journey between Turan and Iran, and metaphorically as the threshold between boyhood and manhood, between common mortal human existence and anointed heroic kingship.

The text of the *Shahnameh* explicitly associates the Arvand, or 'Swift' river of the tale, with the Tigris, and indeed this particular passage is prime evidence in debates concerning the location of the Arvand. Earlier texts are not so clear on this point, however, and thus the exact location of the river in question has been the subject of some scholarly conflict. It is clear from the story of Feridun, however, that the Arvand was a frontier or barrier utilized by King Zohak to protect himself from exactly the sort of invasion intended by Feridun and his army, and thus it represents both a geographical and a spiritual boundary of sorts. The Arvand is Feridun's Rubicon, as it were, after which there is no turning back from his proposed seizure of power, and by crossing the river he enters into mature manhood and the stature of a fully formed epic hero.

Having set his sights upon taking the throne of Iran and casting down the monstrous serpent-shouldered usurper who occupied the high seat illegitimately, Feridun turned towards his object with Kava the Smith at the head of his army, which marched proudly with the

Kaviani banner at its head. When the force reached the Arvand River, however, their progress was checked, and they stopped and sought a way to cross. Feridun found a ferryman and ordered him to shuttle his entire army across the flood. Zohak, however, had commanded his river guards to deny crossing to all but those who showed them a special document embossed with his own seal, and so the ferryman denied Feridun's request. Although enraged by the obstinance of the churlish ferryman, Feridun did not do as we might expect and teach the man manners under the rough tutelage of his *gurz*, the hero's mighty war mace. Instead, Feridun leapt upon his saddle and forded the swiftly flowing river; his followers plunged into the rushing river behind Feridun, and all his army, though mightily drenched, were able to cross. In the Avestan version of this tale, the hero assuages his wounded honour by transforming the ferryman into a bird which may never alight, although the goddess takes pity upon the poor fool. In either case, Feridun and his army ford what seems otherwise an impassable torrent thanks to the divine intervention of Anahita, who allows them to pass, thus marking the hero's passage into manhood and anointing him for kingship.

To one familiar with the Bible, it is hard not to notice at least a slight resemblance between this story and the Mosaic episode of the parting of the Red Sea; an even clearer parallel may be found in the folk sources of the *Shahnameh*. Here, however, the hero Feridun is marching at the head of an army seeking war, not among a tribe of exiles fleeing oppression, although in both cases a divine hand parts the waters before the travellers. Unlike the patriarchal Hebrew God, who uses the waters both to protect Moses and to punish Pharaoh, the goddess Anahita anoints Feridun by means of his passage through the waters. Given the fact that heroes and villains, demigods and demons, all seek the blessing of Anahita on the eve of battle, Feridun's passage through the Arvand takes on the significance of a baptism of sorts. It is certain that it is directly after this crossing that Feridun the untested boy became the mighty hero, and that Feridun's *farr*, or kingly effulgence denoting the right to rule, was to become ascendant as he threw down the tyrant Zohak from the Peacock Throne of Iran. In this context, an earlier episode drawn from folkloric sources concerning the childhood of Feridun is most

This Middle Elamite female figure from 14th–13th-century BCE Iran might well portray an ancient Iranian goddess.

instructive: in this story, the river acts as a protectress much more reminiscent of the Red Sea of Exodus. In this version of events, the father of Feridun is Jamshid, but in both cases the young hero and his mother flee from the bloodthirsty servants of Zohak in a manner reminiscent of the Holy Family's flight from Herod. In the pertinent folktale, Jamshid bids his wife, heavy with child, to flee from the city and to seek a yellow-and-white cow. This cow, which emphasizes the role of the cosmic, bovine nurturer and protector, fords with ease an otherwise uncrossable raging torrent, and those in pursuit are unable to follow. Thus Feridun is able to grow to manhood unhindered, protected by the life-giving goddess symbolized by both river and cow. In addition, a later episode concerning the young Kay Khosrow, another legendary king, also employs this theme of a river crossing as a coming-of-age ritual through which a young boy is anointed as a kingly man thanks to the watery embrace of the goddess. In this case, the sexual purity of the mother of the hero – and hence the boy's own undefiled blood – is a key element of the story, doubly emphasizing both the identity of She Who is Undefiled and that of the Man Who Would Be King.

In a story of the hero's archetypally marvellous origins and unusual childhood, Feridun's nurturing by the mystical cow Barmaya echoes the ancient relationship between the Cosmic Cow and the Original Man of Iranian creation myth. Faranak, Feridun's mother, secured for him the marvellous cow Barmaya, who acted as both the infant hero's playmate and his wet nurse. Barmaya is also a mentor and teacher of sorts to Feridun, and it is she who teaches the hero to walk. After the tyrant Zohak caused Barmaya to be slain, upon reaching manhood Feridun rose up against the evil king seeking to avenge his beloved bovine nursemaid. In order to do so, he called upon the smiths to fashion for him a great club with a cow head at the cudgel-end, and it was with this very club that Feridun defeated the dragon-demon with a single blow; later, he bound the monster beneath Mount Damavand in a way reminiscent of the Binding of the Norse Loki or the imprisonment of the Greek Titans.

The coming of the hero Feridun was foretold in one of Zohak's dreams, and the tyrant attempted, like Herod in the Bible, to forestall the inevitable through the slaughter of innocents; Feridun is thus anointed by prophecy, but – more importantly – he is nursed at the teat of a supernatural cow which clearly evokes the life-sustaining powers of the goddess. Moreover, Feridun's signature weapon emphasizes several related aspects of Iranian mythology, which serve to underscore the hero's intimate relationship with the goddess. The club is the weapon of choice of a host of related Indo-European heroes, a trait perhaps most familiar to contemporary readers through Hercules. Indeed, Gurz, the great cow-headed cudgel, especially in its employment against Zohak, recalls the recurring mythic theme of the Sky God at war with a demonic monster bent on destroying the order of the world. Indra and his struggle with the dragon of Indian myth comes to mind, as does Thor, who utilizes a cow's head in one of his great battles against Jörmungandr, the World Serpent.

In this potent mythic context, the fact that Feridun specifically mentions the slaughter of Barmaya at the hands of Zohak's minions as a reason for his own rise against the evil king is particularly significant, especially as this magical cow that suckled the hero clearly echoes the Cosmic Cow which lived in harmony with the First Man at the dawn of time in the ancient Iranian creation story. This Ur-Cow represents the life-giving and nurturing powers of the goddess herself, and by avenging Barmaya's death, Feridun reflects in heroic epic form the ancient mythic role of the Sky God who resets the balance of the universe and protects, preserves and extends all life through his destruction of the agent of death. That Gurz is in the form of the Cow, the nurturer and the giver of life, is therefore of no little consequence. In this epic version of a much older tale, we can yet discern a distant reflection of the face of the goddess, as well as the strong arm of her champion.

III

The Scourge of the Middle Eastern and Mediterranean Goddess

Genesis

The mythologies we associate with Mesopotamia, Egypt, Greece and Rome have roots in late Palaeolithic and Neolithic settlements such as Kom Ombo and Jebel Sahaba along the Nile, the so-called Natufian sites in the upper Euphrates Valley and near Jericho in Palestine, the Anatolian centres such as Çatalhöyük and Hacilar, and the Helladic and early Minoan cultures in what became Greece. During what scholars call the Neolithic Revolution (between 8000 and 3000 BCE, depending on the place), hunting and gathering gave way to or was complemented by farming, animal husbandry and the technological advancement that created better tools, weapons and building materials. With the development of permanent settlements, religious traditions which usually accompany centralized living arrangements also developed. Eventually what we think of as cities and 'civilizations' emerged, and mythology provided the metaphors by which these civilizations attempted to understand themselves and their places in the world and the greater universe.

The nature of prehistorical or preliterate civilizations and their mythologies can only be surmised by archaeological evidence. It is generally believed that the first great cities were those of the non-Semitic people known by their Semitic conquerors, the Akkadians, as Sumerians. One theory has it that the Sumerians came into what is now southern Iraq from Central Asia in the fourth millennium BCE. and mixed there with an already present people now called the Ubaids, after the ruin of Tell al-Ubaid near the remains of the ancient Sumerian city of Ur. Other famous Sumerian cities were Eridu, Nippur and Unug (Uruk). It was during the Late Uruk Sumerian period (*c.* 3500–3100 BCE) that writing was said to have been invented, marking the beginning of what we can refer to as history, as opposed to prehistory, and historical or recorded knowledge, along with archaeological knowledge. In addition to writing, the Sumerians mastered elaborate sculpture and monumental architecture, a legal system and at least a form of elected religious and civil government. All of these achievements would influence the cultures that followed the Sumerians in Mesopotamia.

By the end of the fourth millennium BCE, not far away, in Egypt, the first great nation-state was well on its way to being developed. The Egyptians, like the Sumerians, were adept at toolmaking and the arts, and they, too, developed writing. They also made boats, allowing them to trade widely in the region, and by the end of the fourth millennium they had established viable governments under pharaohs, beginning with Narmer (3110–3056 BCE) or his son Aha, the two known collectively as Menes, who united northern and southern Egypt, with its capital at Memphis (near present-day Cairo). Later, after the country was once again divided, it was reunited in a third millennium period known as the Old Kingdom. This was the period of the Great Sphinx and the pyramids at Saqqara and Giza.

Further west, on the island of Crete, settlements had been established since about 7000 BCE, and by 3500 BCE signs of what would become known as Minoan civilization were evident. This was a civilization that produced the famous palaces such as the one at Knossos, and it, too, eventually developed a writing system. On the islands called the Cyclades, a parallel civilization had been forming since the middle of the fourth millennium BCE, and on mainland Greece the Helladic culture preceded the Mycenaean one we associate with the events of the Homeric epics. There is ample evidence that all of the above cultures traded with and influenced each other.

In Mesopotamia the various city-states of Sumer tended to fight against each other for supremacy, except when they found it necessary to unite to confront the constant threat of Semitic peoples from the north. The northern threat led to a kingship system which replaced an older system of shared power by a priest-king (the *en*) or a queen-spouse of the city deity, and a military leader (the *lugal*). Several of the kings were celebrated in heroic sagas, such as in the famous myths of Gilgamesh, Enmerkar and Lugalbanda, all kings of Uruk. In about 2370 BCE the Sumerian region was conquered by a semi-legendary king, Sargon I, of the Semitic Akkadians. Sumerians and Semites had fought over the land for centuries before Semitic dominance was fully established with a capital at Babylon, the city where the famous ziggurat known familiarly as the 'Tower of Babel' would later be built. The most famous of the Babylonian kings was Hammurabi (*c.* 1792–1750 BCE), the developer of a code of laws which unified the nation's diverse races. Wars continued in Mesopotamia, however, and in 1600 BCE the Hittites, who had become a major power in Anatolia (modern Asian Turkey) conquered Babylon, only to be displaced by other powers during the later part of the second millennium. Assyrians from the north and Elamites from the east controlled Mesopotamia for a time before King Nebuchadnezzar I (*r. c.* 1125–1104 BCE) re-established Babylonian control near the end of the millennium.

During the struggles for hegemony in Mesopotamia, Egypt was threatened by division. The Old Kingdom came to an end late in the third millennium BCE, and two kingdoms, with capitals in Memphis in the north and Thebes (modern Luxor) in the south, emerged. At the very end of the millennium, the kingdoms were again united as what we now refer to as the Middle Kingdom. In about 1750 BCE, Egypt was invaded by mysterious people known as the Hyksos, and it was not until around 1580 BCE that these invaders were driven out. Now united as the New Kingdom, Egypt became the greatest power in the area under Thutmose I, Thutmose II, the queen-pharaoh Hatshepsut and, especially, Amenhotep III, whose reign, beginning in about 1386 BCE, marked the high point of Egyptian civilization. The artistic achievement of the period was extraordinary and the Egyptian empire expanded into parts of Mesopotamia and Canaan (modern Palestine, Lebanon and Israel). The successor to Amenhotep III was his son, Amenhotep IV, who changed his name to Akhenaton to reflect his support of a change in the state religion to make it focus almost exclusively on a single and all-powerful sun god, Aton (Aten). Akhenaton's major wife was

Nefertiti. His son and heir was Tutankhamen, known to many today as King Tut. The power of Egypt was somewhat diminished when, under the Pharaoh Ramesses II, the Egyptian army was fought to a draw by the Hittites in 1300 BCE.

For some time, Egypt had been more or less in control of the land known as Canaan, where the 'Canaanites', a collection of several Semitic, non-Egyptian tribes – for example, the Edomites, Moabites, Midianites and Ammonites – lived. It is generally believed that a group called 'Habiru' by the Egyptians moved out of Egypt into Canaan in about 1250 BCE. These were the ancestors of the Hebrew people – semi-nomadic tribes who would eventually wrest control of Canaan from the existing population. Important Canaanite centres had been established earlier in the second millennium along the Mediterranean coast, and these had traded widely with the Egyptians and Mesopotamians. Among these Canaanites were the Phoenicians, who invented an alphabet in circa 1500 BCE and are associated with cities such as Sidon, Tyre and Byblos, all in what is now Lebanon. A particularly important Canaanite settlement was Ugarit (Ras Shamra in modern Syria).

The emergence of the Hebrews in Canaan coincided roughly with invasions all over the Middle East by people, probably from the Aegean area, known as the 'Sea People' and associated by some scholars with the Philistines who threatened the Hebrews and the Canaanites. By the end of the eleventh century BCE the various Hebrew clans had united under a monarchy, first represented by the biblical Saul and then by his son David. David was successful in struggles against the Canaanites and Philistines and established a capital at what had been the Jebusite city of Jebus (Jerusalem). After David's death, Solomon became king and built the first great temple of Yahweh there – Yahweh being the god who had for some time been the deity of the Hebrews, now Israelites. In about 928 BCE a civil war led to the division of the Israelite-controlled territory into two lands, Israel and Judah, which were ultimately conquered by Assyrians from Mesopotamia. In 612 BCE the Assyrians were defeated by an alliance of Medes, from Persia, and Babylonians. Once again Babylonians, under King Nebuchadnezzar II of the Chaldean dynasty, ruled the area. This was the period of the famous Hanging Gardens of Babylon and the

This early 20th-century reproduction of a dagger found at Mycenae depicts a lion hunt on one side and a hunting lion on the other.

sacking of Jerusalem, which involved the destruction of Solomon's Temple and the exile of Judaeans to Babylon, where, during their captivity or exile, Judaism, as it was later known, developed.

The wars in Canaan during the second millennium BCE coincided with the wars in the Mediterranean region as represented by Homer's epics. This was also the time of the emergence of Mycenaean power in Greece and Crete. During the eighth century BCE an Anatolian people, the Phrygians, rose in importance under the semi-mythical King Midas. The period marked by the revival of Babylonian power and the exile of the Hebrews coincided with what we think of as the Dark Ages in Greece, followed by the emergence of archaic Greek culture in the Homeric period and the great classical period beginning in the fifth century BCE.

If history begins with writing, history probably began in Mesopotamia. By 3500 BCE the Sumerians, in what is today southern Iraq, had made use of previously developed pictograph symbols to evolve a writing system that used wedge-shaped glyphs pressed into clay tablets. By 2800 BCE that system had become more abstract and more phonological, with signs standing for syllables rather than for objects, thus making it more appropriate for literary activity rather than merely inventory lists. Later, the Semitic Akkadians and Babylonians, and the Anatolian Hittites, adapted it to their own languages. We call this writing system 'cuneiform' from the Latin *cuneus,* wedge, and *forma,* form. The cuneiform tablets give us at least a few aspects of Mesopotamian mythological history. Among the most famous of the cuneiform-related tales are those of the greatest of the Sumerian goddesses, Inanna (later Ishtar). One tablet lists the 'herders and cows in Inanna's fields', while others tell of her descent to the Underworld and her ascent to a position of power over many of the male deities. The two most fully preserved mythic tales that derived from earlier cuneiform texts concern Gilgamesh. These stories were produced on twelve clay tablets sometime between 2750 and 2500 BCE and featured Bilgamesh or Gilgamesh, a legendary king of Uruk, who, according to the Sumerian King List, lived for 126 years and built the walls of Uruk and a great temple to the goddess Ninlil. The stories were incorporated into an Akkadian and still later into Babylonian and Assyrian versions to make the overall work we refer to as the Epic of Gilgamesh, standardized sometime between the thirteenth and tenth centuries BCE. In the epic we find a flood myth which resembles the Bible story of Noah and his Ark. The flood hero of the Babylonian version is Utnapishtim; the Akkadian counterpart is Atrahasis. Both are based on an earlier Sumerian flood hero, Ziusudra. The Akkadians and Babylonians made use of the language and stories they absorbed from the conquered Sumerians, much as the European world has made use of Latin and Graeco-Roman culture. Sumerian and Babylonian tablets and the Sumerian language would remain the religious and literary language of the area long after the Sumerians no longer existed as a culture.

To a great extent, Mesopotamian mythology reflects agricultural considerations in connection with the fertile land around the Tigris and Euphrates rivers and the marshlands in the south. For the Sumerians, especially, sexual imagery served this mythological theme well, and goddesses played a large part in the mythology. The original Great Goddesses of Mesopotamia, whether Ninhursag, or Ki or Kishar, are recognized as necessary for creation itself and are usually associated with earth and its productivity. Among our earliest 'religious' narrative poems are those featuring the goddess Inanna – the embodiment of the land itself, who longs to be fertilized.

Another theme of Mesopotamian mythology, however, especially in the Babylonian version, is the reckless power of the ancient female forces, represented, for instance, by the monstrous Tiamat, who must be destroyed, and the seductive Ishtar (the Babylonian Inanna); her sexuality is resisted by the male hero Gilgamesh, who sees it as a threat to his power. The great work of Babylonian culture is the creation story, the Enuma Elish, which was probably composed in Hammurabi's time but which in the form known to us was included in the Library of King Ashurbanipal in the seventh century BCE. The primary purpose of the Enuma Elish would seem to be to celebrate the rise of the god Marduk, the city god of Babylon, over the earlier Mesopotamian gods and especially over the old female power of his victim Tiamat.

In Egypt, writing came into being just after or simultaneously with that of Sumer. Some Egyptians believed that writing had been invented by the god Thoth, while others said it was the goddess of wisdom, Seshat, who invented it. Egyptian writing developed from the fourth millennium BCE, from simple picture signs to a more complex system known as hieroglyphics (in Greek *hiero* means 'sacred' and *glypho* means 'to carve, engrave'), which were written on temple walls and royal tombs. The glyphs were both semantic and phonetic, simultaneously representing objects and sounds. The writings carved into the walls of the first great pyramids, those at Saqqara beginning in about 2400 BCE during the Old Kingdom, were religious in nature and are known collectively as the Pyramid Texts. Later writings from about 2000 BCE on coffins contained mythological information about the afterlife and the god Osiris, and other mythological themes. These are known as the Coffin Texts. A still later source for our knowledge of Egyptian funereal practices and myths is the *Book of the Dead* (also transliterated as 'The Book of Coming Forth by Day'), which is written on papyrus scrolls and dates from about 1550 BCE. Hieroglyphs remained undecipherable until the Rosetta Stone, a granodiorite stele recording a decree of Ptolemy V in 196 BCE, was discovered in 1879. The presence on the stone of Greek and demotic (popular) Egyptian script alongside hieroglyphs enabled the latter script's translation.

The mythology revealed in hieroglyphs, and demotic Egyptian and later Greek sources, is highly complex. It differs in detail from one cult centre to the other, but in general it focuses on the afterlife ruled by the great king and god Osiris, the sun god Ra, creators of various names and other gods, usually depicted with animal heads. It also gives important roles to several goddesses, including early Great Mother goddesses such as Mut (Mother), Hathor and the sky goddess Nut, as well as more frightening figures such as the lion-headed warrior goddess Sekhmet and the snake goddess Wadjet, and more mystical goddesses such as Isis, the wife and sister of Osiris, and their sister Nephthys.

In Canaan, when the Hebrews arrived from Egypt, they found a culture adept at writing. From about 1400 BCE the people of Ugarit and Phoenicia had a sophisticated alphabet in which letters corresponded to sounds in their Semitic languages. The scripts found in Ugarit temples dedicated to the gods Baal and Dagon were especially rich in mythological material. It was a mythology which, like the Babylonian, emphasized a new patriarchal power, personified here by the god Baal, who struggled against an earlier chaotic force represented by Yam, a sea monster like the Babylonian Tiamat or the Hebrew Leviathan. Goddesses play a significant role in Ugaritic mythology. They include the Great Mother goddess Atirat (Asherah), the wife of El (or of Dagon, the bull-god father of Baal). Baal's powerful sister was Anat, the virgin warrior goddess. She has much in common with Athtart or Astarte ('The Face of Baal') and is an apparent version of the Mesopotamian Inanna/Ishtar.

As for the Hebrews, when they arrived in Canaan and eventually replaced a nomadic lifestyle with an agricultural one, the fertility goddess Asherah became an attractive figure who was even seen at times as the wife of Elohim, the prototype of Yahweh. The Hebrew

These 7th-century BCE baked clay figures of the goddess Astarte, the biblical Ashtoreth, are from a tomb in the vicinity of Bethlehem.

prophets such as Jeremiah saw Asherah, the so-called 'Queen of Heaven', as a threat to the emerging monotheistic religion of the Israelites and, in effect, insisted on a 'divorce', leaving the distinctly unmarried Yahweh, God or Allah that we find in the three major monotheistic religions today.

The Israelites developed a mythological history in their Bible, consisting of the first five books – Torah – and the later books that follow it. Much of the Bible was in all likelihood based on early stories written down during the exile in Babylon and under later Persian rule – that is, between 600 and 400 BCE – and is somewhat influenced by Mesopotamian narratives such as the flood story. Under Rabbinic Judaism, the commentaries in the Talmud added a dimension to the earlier mythology. Christians added the New Testament to the Bible, including four 'biographies' of Jesus and commentaries in the Epistles (letters to the faithful) by Paul and others. Muslims added to the sacred scripture of monotheism with the Qur'an, containing the words of Allah as spoken to Muhammad by the angel Jibril (Gabriel). Goddesses play little or no role in religions that recognize only one god – the divine being almost always depicted in male terms. Only the presence of Mary, a new 'Queen of Heaven', creates a measure of ambiguity on the goddess concept in Christianity. In the Islamic world, goddesses exist only as false figures of the Arabic past, such as the *banat al-Lah* (Daughters of God) mentioned in the Holy Book but eventually dismissed by Muhammad as 'empty names', much as the Hebrew prophets had dismissed Asherah.

In what we think of as the Greek world, writing was first developed in the Cycladic Islands and Crete. A script discovered by archaeologist Arthur Evans existed in the islands and Crete from about 1800 BCE. Linear A, as Evans called this script, consisted of lines pressed into clay. A more picturesque language, consisting of hieroglyphs, developed in Crete beginning as early as 1625 BCE, perhaps influenced by contact with Egypt. Both Linear A and Minoan hieroglyphic writing remain essentially undecipherable and probably were used to represent a now dead Minoan language.

Another type of writing was developed out of Linear A to express a form of Greek language used in Crete and Mycenaean Greece from about 1450 BCE. This writing was deciphered by the English architect and linguist Michael Ventris and is called Linear B. Linear B was used primarily for inventories, or such purposes as lists of gods. There are Linear B versions of almost all of the Olympian gods, for example. After about 1100 and until 800 BCE, however, writing seems to have disappeared in Greece. This period is generally referred to as the Greek Dark Ages and coincides with the period used by Homer as the setting for his epics.

During the Dark Ages there would have been a tradition of oral storytelling by bards such as the blind Demodocus described in Book Eight of the *Odyssey*, a kind of self-portrait if the blind poet we know as Homer ever existed. Working in the eighth century BCE, the poets represented by Homer almost certainly composed their works orally. Although they were probably stabilized by the late eighth century BCE, the *Iliad* and *Odyssey* were not written down in their current form until later. The same is true of the *Theogony* by Hesiod, and the *Homeric Hymns*, attributed to a group of rhapsodes (minstrels) known as the Homeridae.

The mythology of Greece is patriarchal in character, reflecting the realities of Greek culture. The Olympian family is an often comic but sometimes tragic mirror of upper-class society. There is a philandering and arbitrary father; two power-hungry and dangerous brothers who, like him, are sexual predators; a nagging and jealous wife; and a large number of offspring, whose actions, like those of their parents, make for what is, to some extent, a mythology of mini soap operas. Although gods dominate the Greek religion, there are important goddesses, and it is several of these goddesses whose actions take us beyond soap opera to something more profound. Among the most important of these are the Mother Earth creatrix, Gaia; another Earth Mother, Demeter; Demeter's daughter Persephone; and the patron goddess of Athens, Athena.

Greek mythology influenced that of the Romans. It is common practice, for instance, to equate the Olympian family with the family of gods at the head of the Roman pantheon. Thus Zeus became Jupiter, Hermes became Mercury, Poseidon became Neptune and so forth. There are many Roman goddesses, some of them Greek in origin, some Etruscan, and some gleaned from the mythologies of conquered peoples further afield.

Faces of the Goddess

The Middle Eastern and Mediterranean goddess wears many cultural clothes – Sumerian, Semitic, Egyptian, Minoan and Graeco-Roman – but her essence is consistent. She is the Great Mother – even the creatrix – who usually represents Earth in union with the male Sky. She evolves into a dominating queen and sometimes into a terrifying instrument of death as a warrior or seductive underminer of masculine power. She is the mother, the lover and the warrior. She begins her mythological life in prehistory, and some would say she continues to live on in the mythology of our own age.

In the region in question, the mother appears early in figures whose identity and mythology we can only surmise from her physical depiction. In the preliterate Palaeolithic and Neolithic periods there are many examples of opulent, large-breasted, wide-hipped females in sculptures and drawings who could well be goddesses, and who seem to suggest the concept of fertility and motherhood. A good example is the famous tiny terracotta figurine from Çatalhöyük in Anatolia, dating from 6000 BCE. The subject is a woman – assumed by archaeologists to be a goddess – apparently giving birth. She is seated royally on a throne flanked by two feline animals. The 'sanctuary' in which she was found is also decorated with depictions of a bull figure, presumed to be her mate. Other depictions at Çatalhöyük are of the birth of a bull 'god', the sexual embrace of a male and female next to a female holding a baby, and a more frightening picture of the goddess as a vulture in the process of decapitating tiny figures, a prefiguration of the Destroyer Goddess. Another example of the prehistoric 'mother goddess' is the 'Sleeping Lady' of Malta. Still other possible examples in the region are 'goddesses' of Ubaid, the Cyclades and Crete.

All of these figures have exposed breasts and in two cases stylized genitalia, perhaps suggesting motherhood. The Ubaidian and Cycladic figures have snake-like heads, and the Minoan goddess holds two menacing snakes in a display of fearless power. The theme of the goddess who gives but also takes away is at least suggested by these prehistoric depictions. Once we move into the historical period the characteristics of the goddess become more focused.

This Minoan
cylindrical seal
is wrought of
haematite and was
excavated on Cyprus.
It depicts an axe,
a rosette, a tree, lions,
goats, a large winged
ox-head figure, a
shrouded woman
and a small winged
figure, some of which
may evoke ancient
Minoan faces of
the goddess.

In the Sumerian mother goddess myths we find metaphorical
elements that are repeated in creation mythologies all over the world.
These include the birth of life from the primeval maternal waters, the
marriage of Earth and Sky, and the separation of Earth and Sky. In
the beginning, there was Nammu ('Lady Vulva'), whose cuneiform
symbol means 'sea'. As the primeval seas, she gave birth to the god An
(Heaven or Sky) and the goddess Ki (Earth). Joined together, An and
Ki were An-Ki (the universe). From them came the god of Air, Enlil,
who separated An and Ki – Heaven from Earth – thus making space
for further creation. In later myths, Ki takes other mother goddess
forms such as Ninmah, Nintu, Ninmu, Ninhursag and Uttu. Whatever
name the goddess takes in Sumer, she is a vehicle for fertility, new life
and sexuality, which in the Sumerian religion is a positive force, clearly
related to the irrigation of the marshlands of what is today southern
Iraq. The story of Enki and Ninhursag is a good example.

Enki was one of the original gods, a son of Nammu herself. He
was the water and trickster god, and also the god of wisdom. Like
tricksters everywhere, Enki was driven by sexual desire. He filled the

ditches of the marshlands with his semen, or water (the word for both was the same in Sumerian; the life-giving 'semen' of the father god An was rain, and sent it into the womb of the earth mother Ninhursaga, who then gave birth to the earth as Ninmu. He then impregnated Ninmu, who gave birth to Ninkurra ('Mistress of the Land'), who in turn gave birth to Uttu ('Plant Life'). Now Enki desired Uttu, but Ninhursaga urged the girl to be coy, to resist Enki unless he promised her various fruits and vegetables. When Enki produced these, the delighted Uttu took the god 'into her lap' and he poured his semen into her. He 'put his foot into the boat', not planning to 'stay on dry land for long'. 'Foot' here probably means 'penis', and 'boat' 'vagina'. In any case, Ninhursaga wiped the excess semen remaining on the girl and created still more plants.

It is easy to see in these myths how the ancient Earth Mother morphs into the goddess of love who, like Uttu, entices the necessary lover. In Sumer the greatest of all goddesses is the goddess of fertility and love, Inanna (Nin-Ana, Innin), who later, among the Semites, becomes Ishtar. Innana, the patron of Uruk, was the 'Queen of Heaven and Earth' and 'Lady of the Date Clusters'.

It is in a contest with Enki that Innana achieves her dominant position in the mythology of Sumer. Enki engages in a drinking battle with the goddess, who has complained of her secondary position among the gods. It is Enki who controls the sacred *me*, the rules and offices that have controlled the arrangement of culture since creation. In their contest Enki becomes so drunk that he gives up the *me* to Inanna, who immediately places them in her 'boat' (vagina) and flees to Uruk.

In Uruk, Inanna is the ultimate mother longing to be fertilized. She chooses the shepherd Dumuzi (Tammuz) as a mate, and her mother Ningal urges her to 'open' to him. Inanna agrees, prepares her body properly, and calls on her lover to fill her:

My vulva, the horn,
The Boat of Heaven,
Is full of eagerness like the young moon.
My untilled land lies fallow. . . .
Who will plough my vulva?

And Dumuzi, the shepherd, now king, is accommodating: 'I, Dumuzi, the king, will plow your vulva.' And the land burst forth with gardens of fruit and other plants. Dumuzi sings, 'O Lady, your breast is your field . . . Your broad field pours out plants . . .'. The tone of these 'hymns', translated by Diane Wolkstein and Samuel Noah Kramer, reminds us of the love verses to be found in the biblical Song of Songs.

The best-known story of Inanna is that of her descent to the Underworld, a descent made by heroes in the mythologies that sprung up all over the world in later centuries. Innana's return from the land of the dead, where she goes to visit her sister Ereshkigal, Queen of the Underworld and Queen of Death, adds the element of resurrection that links it to later stories such as those of Persephone, Osiris and Jesus. In effect, Innana journeys to discover her dark side, the negative reality of her ripe fertility. Ereshkigal is unfruitful sexuality, Inanna's natural enemy. Innana arrives at the gates of her sister's domain wearing the *me* she had gained from Enki, but Ereshkigal will only allow her to come into her presence if she strips herself of all clothes and ornaments of power, including the *me*. The elements of functioning life – sexual, political, familial, religious – would seem to be useless in the world of death. Inanna, seeking dominance over the worlds of both life and death, tries to usurp her sister's throne and fails. As a punishment, she is killed and hung naked on a wall like a piece of meat.

Back in Uruk, Inanna has been absent for three days, so the people go into mourning. Innana's loyal handmaiden, Ninshubur, begs the gods to free her mistress, but they refuse. Only Enki, the shamanic trickster god, who lives in the underground waters and understands the Underworld, agrees to help. Enki creates two mysterious beings from the dirt under his fingernails and sends them with the plant and water of life to Ereshkigal to comfort her in her eternal negative suffering. He knows she will offer his emissaries a reward for their work. When she does, they demand the return of Innana. The gods of the Underworld will allow Inanna's return only if a substitute takes her place. Enki's two creations revive Inanna with the plant and water of life, and she leaves, gathering up the *me* and her clothes on the way. She is accompanied by demons who will ensure that the payment of a substitute is made. When she arrives at Uruk she discovers Dumuzi ruling happily in her place and angrily condemns him to be her substitute in the Underworld. Dumuzi's sacrifice is somewhat mitigated when his sister agrees to take his place in the Underworld for six months of each year.

Sumerian mythology was absorbed by the Semitic peoples of Mesopotamia, the Akkadians, Babylonians and Assyrians, but by the time of the great Babylonian creation epic, the Enuma Elish, in the twelfth century BCE, Mesopotamian politics had changed, and religion had followed the lead. It was during the reign of Nebuchadnezzar I that the god Marduk was elevated as the City God of Babylon and as the chief of the Babylonian pantheon. In order to achieve this position Marduk had to destroy the power of the Great Mother goddess, who in the eyes of the creators of the Marduk cult and the Enuma Elish was no longer a nurturing mother but instead a terrifying monster.

This conversion began when Tiamat – the maternal saltwaters – merged with the fresh water personified by Apsu and gave birth to the first gods, the 'hairy ones' known as Lahmu and Lahamu. These gods produced Anshar the sky god and Kishar the earth goddess, who in turn generated Anu (the Babylonian version of the Sumerian An) and Ea (Enki in Sumeria). These new gods made so much noise that they disturbed Father Apsu, who determined to get rid of them. Tiamat, however, like the Greek Gaia in her struggle with her mate Ouranos, could not bear to kill her own offspring. It was Ea who helped Tiamat by using his magic powers to send Apsu to eternal sleep in the underground waters, the *apsu*. Meanwhile, Ea and his mate Damkina produced the god Marduk, a gigantic storm deity with four heads, who stirred up huge winds and waves. The resulting noise and commotion so upset Tiamat – once revered as the nurturing mother of all things – that she became the epitome of the destroyer goddess, a monstrous dragon-like figure who led an army with her son Kingu (Qingu) against the other gods. The gods so feared Tiamat that they begged Marduk to lead the fight against the destroyer goddess. He agreed only if they would recognize him as the chief among gods. They agreed, and thus Marduk became the great god of Babylon, who filled Tiamat's monstrous mouth with wind so that she could not devour him and then pierced her huge bloated body with a deadly arrow. Out of Tiamat's corpse Marduk made the world, in effect replacing the old Sumerian creation myth with a new one, in which the ancient mother goddess was still the source of existence but now as a dismembered monster subservient to the patriarchal power. Marduk cut her body in two, making half into the sky and the other half into the earth. Out of her head the new god made a mountain, out of her eyes the Tigris and Euphrates rivers, and out of her breasts the hills of Mesopotamia. Marduk then established the city of Babylon with himself as its chief god, and he instructed Ea to create humans out of Kingu's blood.

In Babylon, Inanna herself, the great goddess of Uruk, became Ishtar, one of – if not the first of – the love goddesses mirrored in a line of deities including Isis, Astarte, Aphrodite, the Irish Morrígan and so many others. No longer the nurturing fertility goddess of the Sumerian tradition, she uses her feminine sexual powers in a way that threatens the patriarchal system. In the Babylonian version of the Epic of Gilgamesh, for instance, she tries to seduce Gilgamesh on his way to accomplishing his life's mission and is treated not with respect by the hero but roughly and dismissively as a destructive and dangerous femme fatale.

The Egyptian Great Goddess takes several forms in the various cult centres. During the Old Kingdom she was often a creatrix associated, like the Mesopotamian Tiamat, with primeval waters. Neith was one such water goddess; Mut was another. In the Old Kingdom mythology, Mut was self-generated, as Gaia was in Greece, and known as 'She Who Gave Birth to Many but was Born of No One'. As Queen of Heaven, she carried the symbols of Upper and Lower Egypt on her crown. Later, in Thebes, she was the maternal aspect of a triad that included the father god Amun and the couple's son, Khonsu. When Amun was assimilated into Ra as Amun Ra during the Middle Kingdom, Mut became Hathor, the cow goddess, a goddess who had existed on her own since the early dynasties as a mother deity. Eventually, Mut took on more warrior-like aspects associated with such figures as Bast, Wadjet and Sekhmet. Still later, Mut-Hathor was absorbed as the great Isis, who formed a triad with Osiris and their miraculously conceived child, Horus.

In this bronze Egyptian figure of the 4th–3rd century BCE, the goddess Isis is clearly identified by the sun disc and cow horns that surmount her cobra-adorned vulture headdress. She offers Horus her left breast using her right hand.

Osiris and Isis were part of the sacred family of nine, the Ennead of Heliopolis, the cult centre near modern Cairo. Their grandmother was the goddess of water, Tefnut, and their father was Shu, god of air. Shu and Tefnut produced the earth god Geb and the sky goddess Nut, who, reversing the usual role of sky god and earth goddess, are oddities in world mythology. As the sky, however, Nut fits the Egyptian vision of the goddess not so much associated with earth-based fertility for humans as with a heaven-based generation of deities and the elements of creation. In this sense Nut, who arches over the universe when she is separated by Tefnut (air) from Geb (Earth), becomes like other depictions of the creatrix mother goddess such as Neith and Mut.

Nut's primary offspring are Osiris, Isis, Nephthys and the wicked Set, who are the cast of one of the greatest of Egyptian myths, that which reflected an Egyptian concern of utmost importance: the passage from life to death, featuring the particular power of the goddess. In the myth, Osiris is the god-king of a golden age Egypt; his queen is his sister Isis. The royal couple's most important companions are their siblings, Set and his sister-wife Nephthys. According to one of many versions of the story, Set, jealous of his brother, tricks him into lying in a beautiful coffin and then throws the coffin into the sea. This loss of Osiris generates the archetypal search by the Great Goddess – in this case Isis – for the lost half of what is, in effect, the wholeness of life. In this sense, in ancient Greece, Demeter's search for Persephone is a related myth. Isis finds her husband and brings his body home, only for him to be murdered a second time by Set. This time Set dismembers his brother and casts him into the Nile, once again initiating the goddess's search. Isis meticulously collects the pieces of her husband's body, reassembles it and, with her sister Nephthys's help, uses spells to revive the king sufficiently so that when she flies over his body she conceives Horus, the new king-to-be, freeing Osiris to descend to the Underworld, where he will reign as king. Isis, as the embodiment, like Mut and Hathor, of the *maat* – the codes of social order, similar to the Mesopotamian *me* controlled by Inanna – will go on to protect her offspring against the death-wielding negativity of the chaotic Set. It is Isis who hides her son from Set in the wetlands of the Delta. It is she who, like the

Virgin Mary in a later mythology, is often depicted suckling her son, who rests safely on her lap.

The Egyptian goddess is not always a nurturer or protector, however. In several myths she takes the form of the destroyer goddess. The clearest example of the goddess in this role is found in the Egyptian flood myth. There was a time when the god Ra – the sun – struggled with the serpent god Apophis, the darkness, for control of life. When the people lost faith in Ra and were tempted by his enemy, Ra became angry and sent his 'Eye', the goddess Hathor, in her form as the goddess Sekhmet, to punish unfaithful humankind. Sekhmet was, like Kali in India, a terrifying figure, a lion-headed purveyor of death. Nothing pleased her more than the sight and taste of blood. Sekhmet destroyed whatever she came across – crops, people, cities. Her work was so thorough and violent that Ra himself became upset; creation was, after all, his work, and Sekhmet was killing his faithful as well as his unfaithful subjects. Even when he begged the goddess to stop what she was doing, she was so involved in her work that she ignored his request. To put a stop to the destruction of his earth, Ra sent down a flood of beer, which Sekhmet drank, and finally she fell asleep. In this way, Ra diminished the power of the goddess.

Goddesses also play a significant role in the mythologies of the Western Semites in Canaan, Israel and Arabia. It is difficult, however, to distinguish between the identities of the various goddesses because of their closely related names and because of their overlapping roles in the traditions that developed in the area. An Ugaritic tablet tells how the creator god El stood by the sea and impregnated two goddesses at the beginning of creation. These two were the activating Shakti-like aspects of divinity. Merging as one, these goddesses were Athirat-Asherah, who is associated with the sea and is Queen of Heaven and 'Mother of the Gods', a depiction of the Great Mother herself. But in the Baal cycle, the stories of the Canaanite storm god – who, like Marduk in Mesopotamia, gained supremacy over older gods – Athirat seems also to be Anat, the Isis-like sister-wife of Baal, who struggles with him against the enemy god Mot (Death, the Set of Canaanite mythology). Anat was eventually fused with the Phoenician Ashtart or Ashtoret (Hebrew Ashtoreth; Astarte in Greek) – 'Baal's Other Self' – to become the love and warrior goddess who has similarities with Aphrodite, Athena and Artemis, as well as with the Mesopotamian Inanna/Ishtar and the Egyptian Isis. When Baal descends into the winter of death which is Mot, it is the goddess who brings him back and renews fertility.

The Baal cycle opens with a struggle between Baal and the sea god Yamm for supremacy over El's creation. Baal, with his sister Anat's help, wins the battle, and the goddess as Ashtart (Astarte) proclaims his dominance. The goddess is so violent in her destruction of Baal's enemies that Baal, like the Egyptian Ra, has to call off his emissary of destruction, eventually using a trick to lure her back to his side. When Baal desires a palace, presumably to symbolize a new creation, the goddess as Anat agrees to bribe the goddess as Athirat-Asherah, El's consort, to get the ancient high god to agree to Baal's wishes. When Baal, celebrating his new storm god dominance, refuses to pay the traditional tribute to Mot (Death), Mot invites him to the Underworld, and Baal, like Innana before him, feels he must descend to that world and experience death. The world becomes infertile. It is only because the goddess – Anat – intervenes, like Isis, that Baal and the world are saved. She becomes the Destroyer, splitting Mot in two, grinding him up and sowing him in the fields. Baal is reborn from those seeds: the miracle of agriculture is performed, dead seed becoming living plants.

The fertility goddess for the ancient Hebrews was Asherah, the natural wife of the storm god who recognized no wife. As noted earlier, the Hebrew prophets saw in the popular agricultural cult of the goddess a threat to the monotheistic Yahweh religion and demanded what was, in effect, a divorce. The wifeless god was also the god of the Christian and Muslim religions which emerged later in the Middle East. Christians claimed to recognize no goddesses, even though the church gradually made the Virgin Mary into what, from the perspective of non-adherents to Catholic doctrine, certainly appears to be a goddess – the 'Mother of God' and 'Queen of Heaven'. The Muslims simply outlawed the old Arabic goddesses such as Manat, Allat (*al-Lat* means 'the Goddess') and al-Uzza, all deities of fertility and love, recognizing no deity but the one God, Allah. A tradition allowing the Arabic goddesses, collectively the *banat al-Lah*, to serve as intercessors persisted, however, even into early Muslim times, as indicated in the so-called 'Satanic Verses' devoted to them, verses generally discredited but said by some to have been spoken by Muhammad himself.

The goddess takes forms more familiar to most western readers in the classical civilizations of Greece and Rome. In his *Theogony*, Hesiod introduces Gaia, the Great Mother of Greek mythology, who was also Earth itself. Archaeological evidence in caves near Delphi indicates that an Earth Mother was worshipped there from prehistoric times, and by 1400 BCE, as the deity Gaia, she was the central focus of that worship. Gaia worship coincided roughly with the pre-eminence of the great snake goddess of Crete and the great goddesses of the Middle East. According to Hesiod, whose work would have been based at least in part on long-standing folk traditions, Gaia was the first being to emerge from the pre-creation void, or Chaos, which can be thought of as space. Gaia as Earth was the basis for further creation. Tartaros, the personification of the place where those in some sense opposed to proper creation – the defeated forces of evil – would be sent next, was followed by Eros (Love), the force of attraction which would inspire the mating required for a continuing process of creation. Gaia gave birth parthenogenically – that is, without sexual intercourse – to the elements of the earth such as Sea and Mountains and, most importantly, to Ouranos (Sky). As in creation myths from almost everywhere, it was the very nature of Sky to cover Earth in an act of cosmic mating – an act of necessary incest. Whereas Chaos gave birth to non-anthropomorphic realities such as Darkness, Night and Death (Thanatos), Gaia with Ouranos produced a variety of beings, a family of twelve known as the Titans and various monstrous beings such as the one-eyed Cyclopes and the Hekatonkheires (hundred-handed giants).

Ouranos had no interest in offspring, however, desiring only to 'cover' his mate, and as each offspring emerged from Gaia, he pushed it back into her, thus preparing the way for the next logical step, which occurs in creation myths in all corners of the world, beginning historically, for instance, in ancient Sumer with the myths of An and Ki and in Egypt with that of Geb and Nut. The covering of Earth by Sky left no space for further creation, so the first parents needed to be separated. In the Greek story, the separation is violent. The Great Goddess, writhing in pain as a result of Ouranos' actions, gave a sickle to Kronos, one of her children hidden within herself. When Ouranos lay down at night on his mate, his son, prefiguring the much later mythology of Freud's Oedipus complex, reached out with the sickle and castrated his father, flinging the genitals into the sea. Out of the resulting 'foam', the goddess of love, Aphrodite, the archetypal sister of Inanna/Ishtar/Astarte/Isis, was born.

Kronos then mated with his sister Rhea, an Earth Mother replica of Gaia, and immediately took on the characteristics of his anti-creation father. Since his children were born of Rhea he ate them, hoping to prevent a child from doing to him what he had done to his own father. Unhappy at the loss of her children, Rhea made an alliance against her husband with the last of her children, Zeus, in what we perhaps see as the continued acting-out of the Freudian myth. To trick Kronos, Rhea substituted a rock for Zeus when Kronos was about to swallow him. Zeus grew up, eventually giving his father an emetic provided by his grandmother Gaia to make him regurgitate his brothers and sisters, who became the first generation of Olympians and the inhabitants of Mount Olympus. They would go on to lead a successful war in heaven against the Titans and monsters.

With the emergence of Zeus and the Olympians, reflecting a strongly patriarchal society in Greece, goddess power was greatly reduced but remained present. Although Zeus's sister-wife Hera is depicted more often than not as a nagging irritation to her philandering husband, a feminine force who tends to take out her anger against the young mortal women whom Zeus has, in effect, raped, there are goddesses who assume greater significance. An important first-generation Olympian goddess is Demeter, whose strong identification with earth as opposed to Olympus makes her a logical archetypal as well as biological descendant of Rhea and, especially, Gaia. But whereas Gaia and Rhea had taken active steps to overcome the power of their male opposites, Demeter is, in our terms, a 'single mother' with limited power. Her much-loved daughter, the virginal Persephone, had been fathered incestuously, according to Hesiod, by Zeus himself. As if the incest were not enough, Zeus gave his brother Hades (Hell) permission to kidnap the child and take her to the

This iconic marble rendering of Athena is a 2nd-century Roman copy of a Greek original by Kresilas from *c.* 430 BCE.

Underworld as his 'wife'. According to the *Homeric Hymn* to Demeter, against this seemingly unlimited male power, Demeter used the only power she had, the power of the destroyer goddess. Distraught and angry over the theft of her daughter, she withdrew from her care of earth, and a golden age of fertility came to an end, threatening the very existence of humanity. In the end, Zeus and his brother Hades were forced to compromise, and Persephone was allowed to return to her mother for part of each year. In Greece the implications of the Demeter-Persephone myth took a feminist form of sorts in the Mysteries of Eleusis, which celebrated the relationship of Mother and Daughter (Kore) and the possibility of overcoming death. The popularity of these mysteries beginning in fifth-century BCE Greece in what was, in effect, a challenge to the patriarchal Olympian religion, have a parallel of sorts in the much later reverence given to the Virgin Mary, before her importance was solidified in such dogmas as the Immaculate Conception, the Assumption and her perpetual virginity.

Three other Greek goddesses are prominent within the pantheon. These are Athena, Artemis and Aphrodite. All three have the power to destroy. When seen in combination, they are mythological descendants of older goddesses such as Inanna-Ishtar, Isis and Ashtart. The most important of these Greek goddesses was Athena. When Zeus had intercourse with Metis (wiliness), she conceived Athena. Zeus swallowed Metis and kept her inside of himself as a source of intelligence, but eventually Metis' child Athena's presence demanded release, and Zeus himself gave birth to her from his head – appropriate, considering that she was the goddess of wisdom. Athena was a virgin and a warrior, a somewhat masculinized version of the old goddess. Her destructive characteristics are clear in Homer's *Iliad*, where she vies on several occasions with the god of war, Ares, and has no qualms about killing. She terrifies all who see her when she holds up her aegis, with its depiction of the frightful head of the monstrous Medusa. But if the Greeks succeeded in substituting masculine for feminine powers in this goddess, they also made her a powerful figure of wisdom and order against arbitrary destruction and violence. The great playwright Aeschylus makes this clear in the final play of his *Oresteia*, when Athena and Apollo establish a new form of social order based on reason rather than on revenge and blood feuds – the old way represented by the terrifying and destructive goddesses the Furies. Athena becomes the patron goddess of the great city of Athens, her statue standing proudly in the Parthenon, the temple built in her honour.

In classical Greek mythology, Artemis was the twin sister of Apollo, fathered by Zeus and born of Leto on the island of Delos. Artemis is included on the Cretan Linear B list of deities and is referred to by Homer as Artemis Agrotera ('of the wilderness'). She is a goddess of animals and the hunt, protector of maidens and virginity, and goddess of mothers in childbirth. She is also capable of destructive violence, as in the famous myth of her confrontation with the unfortunate Actaeon, who was killed as a punishment for having seen the goddess naked and, according to some versions of the story, for having sexually assaulted her. In Apollodorus' version of the tale, Artemis (Diana to the Romans) turned the inadvertently spying young man into a stag so that his own hunting dogs would devour him. In the *Iliad* Homer describes how the goddess, angry at Niobe for comparing herself favourably to Leto, killed the boaster's six daughters while her brother Apollo killed her six sons. Furthermore, Apollodorus reports that Artemis, angry at a slight on the part of a king, sent a huge boar to destroy the king's land.

Another version of Artemis is the Artemis of Ephesus in Ionia (western Anatolia). This is the famous figure with many breasts, which some scholars identify as eggs and others as testicles of sacrificed bulls. The Ionian version of the goddess would seem to link her more closely with the great fertility goddesses of the Middle East such as Isis and Inanna and the Phrygian Cybele. The Artemis of classical mythology has fertility aspects – such as her association with nature and childbirth – but like Athena, she has been somewhat masculinized as primarily a hunter.

Aphrodite is not included in the Linear B list of goddesses, suggesting that she was a late addition to the Olympian family, perhaps an import from the East, a version of the love goddesses such as Inanna, Isis and Astarte. The fact that Hesiod says she was born not of the Olympian family but of the 'foam' formed by the castrated genitals of Ouranos seems to confirm a certain difference in Aphrodite's origins. Homer, however, believed she was the daughter

This 2nd-century BCE marble figure of Aphrodite Euploia, goddess of 'safe journey', complete with swan and a ship's rudder, was excavated at Knossos on Crete.

of Zeus and Dione, thus planting her firmly in the orthodox mythology of Greece. Whatever her origins, Aphrodite in Greece, as the goddess of love and sexuality (with her sometimes-son Eros), was a potentially destructive force. What had been positive sexuality associated with fertility in the Inanna and Isis myths becomes in patriarchal Greece a source of great danger and foolishness. As only hinted at in Gilgamesh's confrontation with Ishtar in Mesopotamia, women and their sexual powers were a threat to men and to women who believed they were immune to sexual madness. When the women of Lemnos scorned the goddess, she caused their genitals to smell so bad that their husbands deserted them. She led the proud maiden Smyrna, who would not worship her, to develop disastrous lust for her own father. It was Aphrodite, after using her power to lure Paris into calling her the most beautiful of goddesses, who led to the Trojan's seduction of Helen and to the mad destruction associated with the Trojan War. Aphrodite happily joined the fighting in that war, even as she acted like a spoiled child of her doting father Zeus. In fact, Aphrodite was also a troublemaker on Mount Olympus. A comic story told by the bard Demodocus in Homer's *Odyssey* describes how the adulterous affair between Ares and Aphrodite is revealed to all the gods when Aphrodite's lame and ugly husband Hephaistos captures the lovers naked, in flagrante delicto, in a net.

The early Romans had goddesses who emerged from various traditions – Etruscan and other Latin tribal religions – and they tended to equate their deities with those of Greece. Ceres was Demeter, Juno was Hera, Minerva was Athena, Diana was Artemis and Venus was Aphrodite. As tempting as it has always been simply to equate these and other Greek and Roman deities, it must be said that the equations are only valid in part. This becomes clearest in connection with the three major Roman goddesses, Juno, Minerva and Venus.

Before the development of the Roman republic, Juno was an important goddess of the Italian peninsula with roots in the Middle Eastern Uni-Astarte, the Great Goddess of fertility, and well into the republican era she stood with Jupiter and Minerva as an equal figure in a dominant triad. She was a goddess of love and fertility, but she was also a goddess with a strong military component and who, like the Indian embodiments of Shakti, provided an essential energy not only to her mate Jupiter but to existence in general. Juno was not at all the nagging wife stereotype generally associated with her Greek 'equivalent', Hera.

Minerva's source in Italy, meanwhile, was the Etruscan and Latin Menrva, a major goddess with Uni, the Earth Mother who became Juno. Always a popular goddess, she later became part of the Roman triad with Juno and Jupiter. Yet although she, like Athena, was a goddess of wisdom born of the father god's head, she never achieved the mythological importance of her Greek counterpart.

Venus, on the other hand, was central to a defining myth of Rome and was a much more serious figure than the flighty and vampish Greek Aphrodite with whom she is commonly thought to be syncretic. As the mother of Aeneas, the legendary founder of Rome popularized by Virgil in his *Aeneid*, Venus plays a role more equivalent in importance to the role of Athena in Greece as the patron of Athens. Even though she is the goddess of love, she urges Aeneas to leave Carthage for his destiny in Italy instead of remaining in the arms of his Dido. This is a Roman goddess of self-control and discipline.

During the later Roman Empire there were deities directly imported to Rome from the colonies. These deities, including goddesses, are not equated with specific Greek figures. One of the most important is the Phrygian Great Goddess Cybele who was popularly celebrated in Rome with her dying son, Attis. Cybele was a version of the *magna mater*, the Great Mother. In her form as Nana, the goddess conceived miraculously when a pomegranate seed entered her, and she gave birth to Attis. Attis was later persecuted by an evil rival and castrated himself under a pine tree. The result of this strange myth was a sacred three-day ritual performed in Phrygia and later more elaborately in Rome. According to Sir James Frazer, a pine tree was cut down and brought to the sanctuary of Cybele in Rome on 22 March. After the tree was wrapped corpse-like in woollen bands and decked with flowers, a young man was tied to the tree and, later, blood was taken from him. The elements of the ritual were 'buried' in a sepulchre in hopes of a rebirth, perhaps in the form of flowers representing Attis himself. It is possible that the Cybele-Attis ritual made another Middle Eastern import eventually as acceptable in Rome. The story and ritual of Jesus, a myth and ritual of resurrection, would gradually achieve hegemony in Rome and the rest of Europe. And over the centuries, a revival of the Great Mother, Mary, the grieving mother and Queen of Heaven, became a central factor in that process.

Sword from 10th-century Europe, probably Scandinavia.

IV

The Battle Lust of the Northern Goddess

Genesis

We are most familiar with the face of the Northern goddess through the visages recognized and recorded by her Scandinavian children. These peoples were illiterate until their conversion to Christianity around the turn of the first millennium, and they are best known to modern readers through records of medieval monks lamenting the scourge of the Vikings. Not all early Scandinavians were part-time pirates and raiders, however, and their culture involved more than shipbuilding, weapon-making and pillaging. It is useful, therefore, to mark this distinction: Scandinavian culture, language and mythology in general we may term 'Norse'; 'Viking', meanwhile, refers to Scandinavian raiders and raiding practices spanning from the late eighth through to the eleventh centuries.

The term 'Viking' most likely derives from *vik*, the Old Norse word for a bay or inlet; to go *i viking*, in the phrase of the day, originally meant signing on for a seasonal raiding adventure during the days of high summer between the planting and the harvesting of the crops at home on the farm. The later, prosperous Vikings would draw more and more followers, eventually developing into 'sea-kings', powerful military and political figures in their own right. These western Vikings conquered or were granted lands in regions from Scandinavia to Sicily, and colonized new territories in Iceland, Greenland and Vinland (North America). Eastern Vikings, known as Rus', founded a principality which ultimately evolved into modern Russia, and they opened eastern trade routes to Constantinople, where

This early 7th-century Anglo-Saxon purse clasp from the famous Sutton Hoo ship burial illustrates the fine workmanship of the period, as well as the importance of animal imagery and complex patterns to the art of the Anglo-Saxons and their Scandinavian cousins.

they formed the personal bodyguard of the Byzantine emperor. The Scottish Isles, the Irish coastal towns and the Isle of Man fell under Viking sway, and a wide swathe of England became the 'Danelaw', a region characterized by Norse influences in language and law which are still discernable to this day. Moreover, in 1016 a Scandinavian king, Cnut, ascended to the English throne.

While the reasons for the sudden and widespread success and enduring legacy of these peoples were many and complex, it is hard to deny that their religion and world view played a role, and it is perhaps for such reasons that the fierce face of the Northern battle goddess, especially in her role as a Valkyrie, is especially well remembered today. As ever, however, the goddess may not be easily reduced to a simple characterization, and in her Northern guise one may glimpse manifold attributes concerning fertility, fecundity, sexuality and sorcery, as well as those denoting destruction, despair and death.

The great paradox of Norse mythology is that, on the one hand, it provides us with the richest available view of Northern European pagan beliefs and rituals, while on the other, most of that material comes to us second-hand, as it were, either through the pens of enemies, proselytizers and foreigners, or through the sepia-tinged view of later generations of ancestor-revering Icelanders. Thus, classical historians, Christian missionaries and monks, and Arab emissaries provide us with shocking tales of barbarous, wild-eyed Northmen, while nationalistic Icelanders regale us with a mythic heritage worthy enough to stand shoulder-to-shoulder with that of Rome or Greece. In the first camp we must include the *Germania* of the Roman historian Tacitus, the *Gesta Danorum* of Saxo Grammaticus, the histories of Adam of Bremen, the *Anglo-Saxon Chronicle* and various eyewitness accounts, such as that of a funeral ritual and concomitant human sacrifice recorded by Ibn Fadlan. In the second camp we find the *Elder* or *Poetic Edda*, a collection of more than thirty poems written down around 1270 but representing much older concepts; the *Landnámabók*, or 'Book of Settlements' of Iceland; various sagas of the Icelanders; and – most notably – the work of Snorri Sturluson, author of the *Prose Edda*.

Written around 1220 as something of a step-by-step guide for poets, the *Prose Edda* is divided into four parts: a prologue; *Gylfaginning*, or the 'Beguiling of Gylfi'; *Skáldskaparmál*; and *Háttatal*. In *Gylfaginning*, Gylfi is a Swedish king who is able to quiz disguised pagan gods about key aspects of Norse mythology. *Skáldskaparmál* comprises a collection of poetic techniques and phrases, while *Háttatal* is a compilation of skaldic verse – that is, of the forms of Norse courtly poetry. Snorri was an important farmer and political figure, and his intrigues against the Norwegian king ended when he was assassinated in his own home in September 1241.

Faces of the Goddess

Perhaps the best-known face of the Northern goddess is worn by the Valkyries, called the *valkyrjar* – 'Choosers of the Slain' – in Old Norse, who are virgin demigoddesses and Odin's emissaries and functionaries upon the field of battle. The Valkyries often give great victories to mighty warriors time and again, only to slay these same warriors and bring them to Valhalla in the end. While selecting daily the cream of the crop of each earthly battle to swell the ranks of the heavenly *einherjar*, the Valkyries also serve mead and pork each evening to Valhalla's chosen warriors, thus emphasizing the traditional role of noble woman as cup-bearer in early Germanic societies. As is amply illustrated by Wealhtheow, queen of the Danes and mistress within the great hall Heorot in *Beowulf*, the function of the cup-bearer establishes and reinforces rank and privilege among warriors based on attributes of honour and heroic deeds. To be served by the virgin *oskmeyjar*, 'wish girls', of Odin himself is the greatest honour a warrior could receive.

The Valkyries belong to a class of female beings known collectively as the Dísir, which seems in some sources to include most feminine spirits of any power, from mighty goddesses to guardians of the dead, to the undead spirits of human women. Moreover, the Valkyries have close associations with Freyja, the most potent of the Norse goddesses, who takes a share of the battlefield dead and who counts among her treasures a feather coat which allows her to fly. Freyja may thus be linked with these battle goddesses, and most especially with the swan maidens of the Völundr/Weland myth. One may note dryly, however, that Freyja lacks the chastity generally associated with the Valkyries.

The handmaids of the All-father Odin are sometimes said to total nine, other times twelve or thirteen, and then again 29 or even an infinite number. Their names, often evocative of battle and tumult ('Screaming', 'Axe-time') may be more literary than mythic. Though originally clearly superhuman, it seems that some earthly shield maidens and princesses may have swelled the ranks of the Choosers of the Slain. Minor death goddesses such as the Valkyries abound in Indo-European mythic traditions, from India and Iran to Ireland and Iceland. More specifically, the Old English term *waelcyrge*, which has the same etymology as *valkyrie*, generally denotes a kind of witch or fury, possibly revealing the earlier Indo-European female death spirit who is devoid of the late Viking Age trappings that transform this being into the familiar form of the wing-helmeted, breast-plated shield maiden – the Anglo-Saxon records are quite disparaging of such figures, describing them as malevolent and demonic. The description of the Valkyries in the Norse sources, however, is generally more positive, as the death they bring is in a way a rich reward for battlefield valour. The Valkyries thus function as a minor or helping form of a goddess of Fate; indeed, *Gylfaginning* makes it clear that the youngest of the Norns or Fates, Skuld ('Future' or 'What Must Be'), rides forth with the Valkyries on their battlefield missions. The poem

Hákonarmál contains speeches by the Valkyries Göndul, 'Magical One', and Skögul, 'Battle', which explicate the role of Odin's shield maidens as battle Fates, and thus perhaps reinforce the association between the Valkyries and the Norns. The clearest reference to the Valkyries as a form of the Fates comes from *Njáls saga*, in which a vision is described which casts the Valkyries as weavers foretelling the carnage of the Battle of Clontarf in Ireland in 1014. The weft and warp threads tied to the loom were wrought of human intestines, while men's heads served as the weights; the beater was a sword and the shuttle an arrow. The weavers sang a grisly song of the gore and slaughter depicted on the gruesome tapestry woven by the Valkyries.

Primary sources containing references to the Valkyries include most of those texts detailing the entourage of Odin and the afterlife in Valhalla, perhaps most notably *Grímnismál* and *Gylfaginning*, as well as two tenth-century poems in praise of fallen kings: *Eiríksmál*, written after the death of King Eric Bloodaxe at the Battle of Stainmoor in England in 954 CE, and most especially *Hákonarmál*, written in praise of King Hákon the Good after his death at the Battle of Fitjar, on the island of Stord in Norway in 961. The extant versions of *Hákonarmál* include a full transcription in *Heimskringla*, Snorri Sturluson's history of Norway's kings. *Hákonarmál*, although longer and much more fully articulated in its treatment of the Valkyrie theme than *Eiríksmál*, seems to owe a substantial debt to the poet who composed the earlier poem; this is perhaps not surprising, as Eric Bloodaxe and Hákon the Good were both sons of Harald Fairhair, and so their lives were bound to invite comparison. Because Odin's handmaidens choose which warriors will die and when, it is thus natural that they would invite comparison with the Norns.

The number of the Norse Fates is not entirely clear, although they are mentioned and described in a large number of sources. In *Gylfaginning,* Snorri first names three individual Norns and then elaborates on the many other varieties of these figures. The three he calls by name are Urd ('Fate'), Verdandi ('Present') and Skuld ('Future'), and they live near the Well of Urd at the foot of a root of Yggdrasil, the great World Tree of the Norse cosmos. Here they tend to the World Ash and determine the fates of gods, men and all other creatures. The Old Norse word *urd* (*urðr*) is cognate with the Old

English term *wyrd*, and thus is directly related to our modern word 'weird', which gave Shakespeare his 'Weird Sisters', or soothsaying witches, of *Macbeth*.

The Norns manifest a terrible kind of beauty, as they embody both man's hopes and his fears for the future. As Snorri assures us, there are both good and bad Norns, and some are descended from the gods, some from the elves and some from the dwarfs. Some Norns are associated with childbirth, and thus with reproductive, life-giving powers, and the three who are caretakers of Yggdrasil keep the cosmos in balance. The Norns are sometimes also associated with weaving, as is the goddess Frigg, although sometimes the Valkyries are given this task; in any case, the loom is clearly associated with fate, as is, in some cases, the cutting of notches in wood, which may refer both to the mystical practice of rune writing and to the practice of marking time by notching frames and lintels. The Norns, like the Valkyries, may have been related to or even in some measure derived from the Dísir, a sort of catch-all term for a number of female demigods, of which some were patrons of the living, others guardians of the dead or battle goddesses. The destructive power of the *norna dómr*, the 'Doom of the Norns', in any case explicitly emphasizes the life-taking power of the Norns, and thus aligns them with destroyer goddesses such as the Valkyries. The Norns have typically been associated with the Fates of the classical world – the Moirai of the Greeks and the Parcae of the Romans – and this probable link may well point to an ancient provenance, as well as to later literary influences.

Aspects of the Great Earth Mother fertility goddess are represented by several deities in the Norse pantheon, including most notably Jord, 'Earth', identified as the mother of Thor and the consort of Odin, as well as the more familiar Frigg, from whom the word Friday arises, who is the mother of Baldr and was the chief consort of Odin by the literary period. The earliest fairly complete information available describing an earth goddess concerns Nerthus, who has been transformed into Njörd by the time of the Viking Age; Sif, the wife of Thor, and Idun, the keeper of the Golden Apples of Youth, both manifest major attributes of fertility goddesses as well. The two most significant goddesses in the surviving literature of Norse mythology are, however, Frigg and Freyja, and there is some reason to believe that the two may offer different faces of what was once the same deity: *frigg* means 'love', and the Romans equated her with Venus; thus she is associated with the sexuality and pleasure we might be tempted to attribute to Freyja.

Furthermore, while Frigg clearly is designated as the wife of Odin, Freyja is said to have a husband named Od, whose name is cognate with Odin and who often (always, it seems) is away. Moreover, authors including Saxo Grammaticus and Snorri Sturluson accused Frigg, like Freyja, of the easy virtue and transgressive sexuality one would associate with a fertility goddess. In any case, from earliest times an Earth Mother goddess was worshipped as the mate of a Sky Father god, and Frigg clearly was revered in that regard: indeed, a multitude of place names involving compounds of *frigg* make it clear that her cult was active and widespread. Frigg was also the goddess of the loom, and thus was said to have the ability, like that of the Norns, to discern the fates of men. Frigg would sometimes interfere in the enacting of such fates as well: in disputes with Odin concerning their particular favourite mortals, Frigg was not above resorting to the kind of trickery we might expect of the one-eyed god Odin himself. The most important myths concerning Frigg are those surrounding the death of her son Baldr, however, and thus are best dealt with in a discussion of the conclusion of the Norse mythic cycle. References to Frigg are not uncommon, but for details of her sexual promiscuity, see Saxo's *Gesta Danorum* and Snorri's *Ynglinga saga* in his *Heimskringla*: Loki references her incestuous unions with the brothers of Odin in the *Poetic Edda* poem *Lokasenna*, which, along with *Gylfaginning*, is a source of our knowledge that she is a seeress; the *Grímnismál* also contains an example of the disputes of Frigg and Odin.

Stories of the relationship of the goddess to forces of vitality and fecundity, on the other hand, have much to teach us about the starkness of the Norse view of the natural world. For example, the myth of the kidnapping of Idun and the Theft of her Apples of Youth invites a re-examination of the role of the giants as adversaries to the forces of life and vitality embodied by fertility goddesses. The story begins with Loki in the role of boon companion to Odin, but soon we see evidence that the forces of chaos have begun to unravel that relationship. One day Odin, Hoenir and Loki determined to go forth together in search of adventure, and after a long march they found and slayed an ox and built a fire beneath it in order to roast it. As time passed, however, it became clear that some magical force was keeping the ox from cooking, and the gods were perplexed by this turn of events. From high up above them in a tree a mighty eagle called down to them, informing them that it was he who had bewitched their supper, and offered to undo the charm if he were offered his fair share of the meat. The gods assented to this demand, but when the eagle ripped off most of the best meat from the carcass, Loki became angry and struck at the bird with a staff; the blow stuck where it landed, however, and Loki's hand stuck to the staff; thus by the eagle's magical powers Loki soon found himself a most unwilling passenger on a high-speed, low-level flight across the most rugged terrain the eagle could find. Bashed and battered by every stone and stump in the line of flight, Loki feared that he would soon be broken into bloody bits, and he cried out for mercy. In return for his freedom, Loki was forced to swear an oath to deliver Idun and her Apples of Youth outside of the safety of the domain of the gods; this the Trickster did, and he soon made his way more tenderly back the way he had been brought.

Upon his return to Asgard, Loki found it easy enough to trick Idun into coming with him on a search for the most fabulous apples ever seen. The crafty one told the goddess to bring her own Gold Apples for comparison. At the appointed time and place, he handed her over to the claws of the eagle, who was in fact the giant Thjazi in disguise. The gods soon noticed Idun's absence and lamented her departure, as they began to wither and age. When it was determined that Loki was the last one seen with the missing goddess, the gods threatened him with certain and painful death if he did not undo his mischief; to this Loki tremblingly agreed, with the condition that Freyja lend him her feather cloak, which imparts upon the wearer the guise and flight of a bird of prey. Loki soon winged his way to Thrymheim, Thjazi's home, where he found the giant out and the goddess eager to return to her home; transforming Idun into the semblance of a nut, Loki sped for home as fast as Freyja's wings could take him. He left not a moment too soon, however, as Thjazi almost immediately returned home, realized that Idun was missing, donned his eagle guise and flew after the retreating Loki. The eagle was much more powerful than the falcon, however, and soon Thjazi had gained much of the distance between them; the gods were watching for Loki's return however, and as he raced over the walls of Asgard they kindled a mighty blaze that Thjazi, in his great rush, was unable to avoid. The feathers burned from his back and the giant plunged to the ground, where the gods quickly dispatched him. Thjazi's daughter Skadi, meanwhile, waited in vain for her father's return.

In this tale, Loki's role as less than trustworthy is emphasized in his deception of the credulous Idun, and in his willingness to betray the life-giving treasure of the gods we see intimations of the ultimate betrayal to come. Shape-shifting is also emphasized in this myth, and likewise provides a cautionary tale about the misuse of such powers. There is an obvious parallel between the Apples of Youth of Idun and those of the classical tradition, and it seems that these traditions may stem from a common source; indeed, a number of close parallels in the Irish tradition support this argument. Apples and nuts have a special place in Irish myth from earliest times as harbingers of eternal life, perhaps because they contain the mysterious power to sprout forth new life; it may be of special interest, then, to note that Snorri added the details of Idun's transformation into a nut from an unidentified source. Apples and nuts have been identified among grave goods and in graven images in the northern world since at least the classical period; apples may have been linked to the otherworld in Anglo-Saxon England, and the Viking Age Oseberg burial ship contained a bucket of apples. The name Idun signifies eternity and continual replenishment, marking the goddess and her apples as symbols of fertility and the life force itself. Hence Thjazi's attempt to capture and contain this life force is not only an attempt to destroy his enemies, the gods, but another reminder of the role of the giants as personifications of the forces of destruction and chaos which constantly threaten to overwhelm the powers of creation and order. The kidnapping of Idun and the Theft of the Apples of Youth ultimately comes from *Haustlöng*, a skaldic poem by Thjodolf of Hvin credited by Snorri as his main source in his retelling of the tale in the *Skáldskaparmál* section of the *Prose Edda*.

In the myth of the Shearing of Sif, Loki takes a more direct role in meddling with one of the goddesses, this time acting entirely of his own volition, and to no discernable end but to wreak havoc. Although the prank that sets the story in motion seems relatively harmless on the surface, the trickster's demonic mirth bespeaks darker deeds to come. Despite the gods receiving mighty weapons through Loki's quest to compensate Sif for her loss, none of these gifts will avail their owners enough to save them in the final battle of Ragnarök. Loki's use of shape-shifting and his duplicitous interpretation of agreements in this myth also flesh out our growing understanding of his volatile character.

Skulking about and acting when no one was aware, Loki sheared the hair of Sif out of pure malice. Once Thor had discovered what Loki had done, he threatened to break every bone in the trickster's body. In the face of Thor's rage, the prankster swore to replace Sif's hair with waves of flowing, growing gold. In order to save himself, Loki convinced the sons of Ivaldi the Dwarf to fashion this hair from gold; they also made Gungnir, Odin's spear, and *Skidbladnir*, the ship of the god Frey, brother of Freyja. The dwarfs gained little but the goodwill of the gods for their labours, but the treasures they produced were magical and beautifully crafted. Loki displayed these masterpieces to Brokk the Dwarf, and the trickster wagered his own head that Brokk's brother Eitri could not fashion three greater treasures. The dwarfs accepted this bet, and Brokk handled the bellows as Eitri fashioned the crafts. Three times Eitri warned Brokk not to dawdle at the bellows, and three times Loki, in the form of a pesky, biting fly, attempted to distract Brokk from his task. The first time, the fly bit Brokk on the arm, disturbing him not at all, and Eitri crafted Gullinbursti, Frey's golden boar; the second time, the fly bit Brokk on the neck, barely annoying him, and Eitri created Draupnir, Odin's Ring of Plenty; the third time, the fly drew blood between Brokk's eyes, causing him to let go of the bellows for an instant, and Eitri produced Mjölnir, Thor's hammer, although the dwarf claimed that his work was nearly ruined, and the handle clearly was a little short.

Brokk and Loki travelled on to Asgard, where the six treasures were placed before the gods, who were called upon to determine the winner of the wager for Loki's head. The golden hair cunningly crafted by the sons of Ivaldi rooted instantly to Sif's head, restoring her beauty, and Odin and Frey were very pleased with the attributes of Gungnir and *Skidbladnir*, just as they were with those of Draupnir and Gullinbursti. The gods were all captivated, however, with the hammer Mjollnir, which promised to be their greatest protection against the incursions of the Frost Giants; thus Brokk and his brother were declared the winners of the wager, and the dwarf called for Loki's head. The trickster tried to offer a ransom to save his life, but when Brokk dismissed this offer out of hand, Loki sped away upon his magic shoes, traversing the sky and the sea. When the dwarf called upon the Thunder God for justice, Thor himself ran Loki to the ground and delivered him for judgement. Just as Brokk moved to take his winnings by cutting off Loki's head, however, the Sly One argued that the dwarf had a right to the trickster's head, but not to the neck. Disgusted but undeterred by Loki's cleverness, the dwarf acted upon the head that he had won and sewed Loki's lips together, presumably so that the trickster might choke upon his own false words, honeyed though his tongue might be.

While on the surface this myth may seem to relate only tangentially to Sif and her hair, the Shearing of Sif is the catalyst that incites the creation of the great treasures of the gods; more to the point, it seems no coincidence that the greatest treasure produced in the course of this myth, the mightiest weapon of the gods in their struggle against the giants, is the phallic hammer which embodies the power and vitality of the husband of the violated fertility goddess. Sif, 'related by love', is the wife of Thor, and references to her are usually in regard to this relationship; as the veneration of Thor by farmers became more and more widespread, his consort may have developed as a tandem deity, and thus the pair might be seen in the light of the classic pattern of Sky God mated with Earth Goddess. Whether Sif always displayed the fidelity attributed to her name is called into question when the goddess is condemned for unfaithfulness by Loki in *Lokasenna*; then again, the trickster accused most of the goddesses of the same or worse.

Still, the question of how Loki had access to the person of Thor's wife in order to cut her hair while she ostensibly slept is an intriguing one in this context, although to a shape-shifter like Loki, this task might not prove overly difficult. Loki's relationship with the forces of chaos may be easily inferred by his impish impulse to steal – for no reason except to cause mischief – the golden hair of a goddess of fertility, hair which might well be likened to golden waves of grain. His playful crime has a dark undercurrent, foreshadowing the trickster's ultimate betrayal of the fecundity and life force of the gods in his plot against Baldr, whose own eyelashes are themselves compared by Snorri to sun-bleached grass. While it has been argued that there is no direct evidence of a cult of Sif and that her name in fact refers to a variety of moss, the image of the goddess's hair magically renewed evocatively reflects the annual miracle of the growth of the new grain crop which undulates rhythmically in the gentle breeze of the growing season. Sif's hastily shaved pate conversely might be likened to a field of stubble as the cold winds blow across it after the harvest. Most importantly, it is often overlooked that the gods gained their greatest treasures precisely because of the consequences of this shearing episode, and one wonders if the relationship between a surplus of agricultural plenty and the opportunity to obtain manufactured goods such as those represented by the treasures of the gods was lost on the audience of the myth.

When the giant Hrungnir grew drunk and boastful in the company of the gods, it was Sif and Freyja he threatened to steal away with him, articulating once more the constant threat of the forces represented by the giants to swallow up the powers of fecundity and sexuality embodied by such goddesses. Snorri provides the fullest telling of the myth concerning Sif's hair in the *Skáldskaparmál* in his *Prose Edda*, in the section in which he details how the gods came to possess their greatest treasures, perhaps thus underscoring the relationship between the potency of fertility and the magic associated with those valuables.

Njörd is another god associated with fertility; moreover, this figure is properly examined in the context of the goddess and changes to her visage. Njörd seems to have been derived from the ancient Germanic goddess Nerthus, the worship of whom is described for us by Tacitus in his *Germania*. Tacitus glossed the name of the goddess as *terra mater*, or Mother Earth, though her cult existed many centuries before the Viking Age; she clearly seems a great goddess fertility figure related to the family of the Vanir, and the early Germanic name Nerthus is certainly cognate with the later Norse Njörd. (The Vanir is the group of Norse fertility gods; the other pantheon, the Æsir, are war gods. Originally, the two groups had been in conflict, and the Æsir both desired and loathed the forces of fecundity and sexuality wielded by the Vanir.) It also seems highly likely that the cults of Frey and Freyja appropriated many aspects of the rites of their forebears. The goddess Nerthus dwelled in a ritual cart which was covered with a sanctified cloth and kept in a sacred grove upon a holy island; none but the high priest of her cult might look upon or touch the cart, the cloth or the *numen*, 'god-head' (presumably the goddess herself or at least her earthly representation) therein, on pain of death. When the cycle of the year had turned to the moment deemed by the goddess to be most propitious, she would embody her shrine within the cart; her priest would divine her presence and would then hitch the cart to a yoke of cattle and take Nerthus forth to visit her followers, although the goddess would remain sequestered and veiled within her sacred wagon at all times. This peregrination marked a festival of peace, calm and tranquillity: all weapons were put up for the duration of the sacred procession, fighting was strictly forbidden and objects of iron were locked securely away. All who received the goddess feasted and rejoiced in peace and harmony until the goddess returned to her home upon the holy island. Then the cart, the cloth and the goddess herself, if it is to be believed, were washed in the sacred waters surrounding her home; once the temple-wagon had been properly cleansed and reassembled, the slaves who performed these tasks were sacrificed to the goddess by ritual drowning in the same waters. The cult and shrine of Nerthus were thus imbued with a sense of terrible awe and sanctified ignorance, since the uninitiated must not survive the sight of her holiest of holies.

Tacitus places the sanctified homeland of Nerthus upon a holy island in the sea, which has been suggested to have been located in the Baltic. Subsequent followers of related cults seem to have practised their worship upon islands in inland lakes, and in marshy or boggy areas. Like Artemis, Nerthus appears to have been a virgin goddess whose nakedness was never permitted to be violated by profane eyes. Tacitus notes the use of boar masks in similar rites, which may provide a suggestive link to the association of these animals with both Frey and Freyja; the boar is in any case associated with fecundity among the Germanic peoples and many of their northern neighbours, including the Celts. Ritual carts and related artefacts of the type described by Tacitus and dating to late antiquity have been found in the bogs of Denmark, and a cart and tapestries unearthed in the great Viking Age ship burial at Oseberg may also represent related rites. Tacitus identified the Angles as one of the tribes which worshipped Nerthus, and thus it is possible that this deity travelled to Britain with that tribe; it is certainly true that charms associated with the Earth Mother were common in the Anglo-Saxon world, as were representations of pagan fertility figures such as Sheela-na-gigs. If Njörd is indeed the late Norse manifestation of the earlier Germanic Nerthus, the transformation of Earth Goddess into Sea God may explain in some measure the suggestion that Frey and Freyja were the fruit of an incestuous union: perhaps this mythic understanding stems from the historical fact that the twin fertility god and goddess were ultimately derived from a single source in the form of Nerthus, a much older and perhaps hermaphroditic Germanic fertility figure. The main source of information concerning the cult of Nerthus is Chapter 40 of the *Germania*, but it is noteworthy that a number of archaeological finds contain ritual carts which may somewhat substantiate the literary record. Many of the ritual aspects described by Tacitus seem to have been appropriated into the worship of Frey and Freyja, and some commentators further note that the classical record offers a Syrian counterpoint in the figure and worship of Cybele, also a fertility deity.

Freyja, or 'Lady', came to the Æsir from the Vanir and, as this origin implies, is an archetypal fertility goddess. Freyja is the sister and perhaps lover of Frey, or 'Lord', as well as both the daughter and niece of Njörd, who begat the twin fertility deities upon his own sister. Fertility and sexuality of all kinds is permitted and even promoted among the Vanir, who tap the rich wellspring of life force in any and all of its manifestations; the taboo of incest and the forbidden magic of *seid* (*seiðr*, a fountainhead of feminine natural forces wielded with abandon by the Vanir but considered transgressive by the hyper-masculine Æsir) both represent the power and the mystery of giving free reign to desire. Indeed, it is the very licentiousness of the Vanir, coupled with the forces released through the embrace of such forbidden pleasures and powers, that the Æsir simultaneously loathe and envy. Freyja is the wife of Od, who is often away, and for whom she weeps tears of red gold; Od is sometimes associated with Odin, but it is true in any case that Freyja is hardly a faithful wife. Freyja and Od have a daughter called Hnoss ('Gem'), who sparkles like a diamond; gemstones take their name from her, and her glittering visage is no surprise as Freyja is herself the most beautiful of the goddesses, as well as the most promiscuous: her rampant sexuality is both representative of and perhaps a catalyst for agrarian fecundity. Love songs are dear to Freyja, and it is wise to solicit her help in romantic affairs.

The darker side of Freyja's character is exemplified by the violent death and destruction of war, which is the opposite side of the coin of unbridled passion that she manifests: uncontrollable sexual urges are not so very different, we are perhaps called upon to understand, from blind bloodlust – it is likewise self-evident that the former are often a trigger for the latter. As an aspect of her role as a war goddess, Freyja claims a share of the battlefield dead, and in this way she manifests a Valkyrie-like attribute; her falcon-feather flying coat further reinforces this association, although it is clear that the hot-blooded Freyja is not cut entirely from the same cloth as Odin's virginal battle goddesses. Odin himself, of course, lusts as much for Freyja's prowess at *seid* as for her voluptuous body. Freyja is, however, without a doubt the object of desire of most males who gaze upon her, including the giants, such as Thrym, Hrungnir and the mason who built Asgard's wall, all of whom represent the forces of chaos which covet and would steal away the gods' powers of fertility. Freyja's vehicle is a chariot drawn by cats, and her home is Sessrúmnir, 'Roomy-seated', which is situated in Fólkvang, 'Folk-field.' Her mode of transport reminds us again of Nerthus, of course, and some have seen in such replicating earth goddesses a pattern reaching back as far as the Near Eastern goddess Cybele, whose cart was pulled by lions. More to the point, it has been suggested that the incestuous links between Njörd and his children in fact evoke the true nature of their hidden relationship: they are all, in reality, different faces of the same deity.

Freyja's falcon-feather coat implies a spirit journey: she manifests attributes of a shamanic shape-shifter and seeress, whose spirit can take flight and return with secret knowledge. In this way she shares traits with Odin, and it is noteworthy that each of these gods serves also as a deity of the dead. Furthermore, animal-skin or bird-feather garments and ritual objects might well be seen to be associated with the magical practices and soothsaying rites we might gather together under the rubric of *seid*. Freyja, we are informed by Snorri, served among the Vanir as a high priestess of the arts of *seid*, and she was the first to teach these rites to the Æsir. Although it is clear from various sources that Odin was a willing pupil of these practices, it is equally clear that this was the form of magic most closely associated with women, and that its practice was considered suspect, at best, among the Æsir. Although it is apparent in the accounts of the war between the Æsir and the Vanir that *seid* could be destructive, most of the rites seem to have involved divination, especially concerning matters of the field and of the heart, the two domains in which Freyja reigned supreme.

This copper-alloy openwork brooch from 11th-century Norway displays an animal figure typical of the Urnes style, which combines zoomorphic forms with interlace.

It is intriguing that Snorri informs us that Freyja was the last of the surviving Norse goddesses, and there is reason to believe that aspects of her cult we would associate with *seid* rituals survived well into the Christian period in the northern world. Certainly the proliferation of place names associated with the goddess throughout Scandinavia bear out her widespread popularity. From various sources, it appears that *seid* rituals most often involved a seeress, called a *völva*, a term meaning 'prophetess' or 'witch', which may refer to the staff or wand sometimes used in such a rite; the most famous mythic example of such a figure is the eponymous *völva* of the Eddic poem *Völuspá*, the title of which means, literally, the *spá*, or 'prophecy', of the seeress. Odin himself called forth this seeress and compelled her to utter her prophecy, again underscoring that god's penchant for gaining hidden knowledge through forbidden activities. In general practice, *völva* rituals seemed to have involved a raised platform upon which the seeress served as officiate, often surrounded by a chanting ward-circle of women. *Seid* practices are associated in some sources with curses and maladies, of course, as well as with shape-shifting (most especially into the figure of a horse), in which guise, presumably, one might crush one's enemies. Generally, however, these rituals seem associated with divination, especially concerning crops, famine, pestilence and personal destinies, as well as in evoking blessings of health and fertility upon crops and people alike.

Perhaps one of the most instructive of the examples of such rites is preserved for us in *Eiríks saga rauda*, the Saga of Erik the Red, which famously discusses the Greenland settlements and reports of the travels of Leif the Lucky, son of Erik the Red, to Vinland in North America. In Greenland during this time there lived a *völva* by the name of Thorbjörg, the last of a group of ten seeresses. Thorbjörg made it her practice to travel from farm to farm during the winter months, predicting for those who invited her what would become of their lives and farms over the course of the coming year. Times had been tough of late, the hunting was scarce, and quite a few hunters had been lost to the wilds. The responsibility of determining when times would improve fell upon the leading farmer in each district, and so Thorkel invited Thorbjörg to visit his house and made arrangements to entertain her with appropriate honours: these preparations included devising a high seat for the *völva*, complete with a cushion stuffed with chicken feathers. Thorbjörg arrived clad in a black mantle with a bejewelled hem, a black lambskin hood lined with white catskin, white catskin gloves and calfskin boots, and holding a staff with a brass finial set with stones. The seeress wore a string of glass beads and carried at her waist a bag of charms necessary to perform her rites; she was belted with a linked girdle. The wise woman was greeted respectfully by all present, was asked to look over all of the people, animals and buildings comprising the farmstead, and then was seated upon her high seat, where she was served a gruel of kid's milk and a stew of heart flesh culled from all the kinds of animals available. After her meal the *völva* rebuffed any questions and took her rest.

As evening fell the next day, preparations were made for the divination ceremony, all items necessary for the ritual were gathered, and the *völva* called out for women who knew the ancient ward chants necessary to proceed. At first it appeared that no such women were present, but eventually it came to light that Gudrid, a Christian, had learned the proper chants at the knee of her foster mother in Iceland. Although Gudrid attempted to refrain from participating in these pagan rites because of her Christian faith, the host prevailed upon her, and finally she consented. The *völva* took her seat upon the raised platform, the women formed a circle about her, and Gudrid drew the spirits to the *völva* through the beauty of her chanting. The *völva* commended her for this, and reported that the poor seasons and long sickness that had harried the colony were at an end; she also predicted a brilliant match for Gudrid in Greenland, and that a long and prosperous line of descendants would spring forth from that union, which would be transplanted to Iceland. The *völva* had good answers for all who questioned her, and, so the saga claims, little she foresaw failed to come to pass. This saga, which preserves a pagan *seid* ritual, also treats the topic of the conversion of Greenland to Christianity: Gudrid is a professed Christian who only hesitantly acknowledges her childhood indoctrination into the heathen rites. We are also informed that this seeress is the last of a sisterhood of ten, and there is some evidence that such practitioners might have travelled in groups until the demise of the cult under the growing pressure of Christianity. Gudrid's reluctant participation in a rite presided over by the ageing

This 11th- or 12th-century Norwegian copper-alloy belt fitting features two horse heads, underscoring the importance of animal figures to Norse ornamental styles.

lone survivor of a ritual group speaks eloquently of the slow demise of this cult during the course of the Middle Ages. The catskin gloves and lining of the hood of the seeress evoke Freyja's link to cats, while the feather stuffing of the cushion provided for the seeress might provide a somewhat more tenuous link to the feather cloak of the goddess.

Perhaps the most well known of the myths in which Freyja plays an active role is that which recounts her acquisition of the Necklace of the Brísings, a treasure associated with a number of sagas and tales of the northern world; this precious object links the goddess to an ancient tradition that associates fertility goddesses with

This 5th-century gold pendant found in Suffolk most likely originated
in Jutland or southern Scandinavia. The images combine the Romulus and
Remus myth of Rome with Norse runes which reference the she-wolf of the
classical myth. This blending of cultures underscores the duality of the goddess
in both mythologies: she is nurturing life-giver at the same time that she is
ravenous life-taker.

necklaces. *Brísingamen*, meaning either 'necklace/girdle of fire' or
more probably the 'necklace of the Brísings', is referenced in several
Old Norse sources, the earliest of which is thought to be *Húsdrápa*,
a tenth-century skaldic poem by Ulf Uggason which is discussed
in *Laxdæla saga* and cited by Snorri in *Skáldskaparmál* and
Gylfagynning of the *Prose Edda*; the necklace is a key identifying
attribute of Freyja in *Thrymskvida* in the *Poetic Edda*. Heimdall is
linked to the necklace in that poem, when he suggests that Thor
wear it as a key component to the Thunder God's drag costume, and
elsewhere Heimdall and Loki are said to have clashed over the
necklace. Most of the detail concerning Freyja's gain and Loki's theft
of the necklace is preserved, however, in a Christianized version of
the myth recounted in *Sörla tháttr* in the Icelandic *Flateyjarbók*
(*Flatey Book* or Codex Flateyensis). The necklace is referred to as

Brosinga mene in *Beowulf,* and in it Háma (Heimir) is said to have stolen it from the hall of Eormenric.

In the fullest version of the myth of Freyja and the Necklace of the Brísings, we are told that one morning, leaving under cover of the dawn mists, the goddess departed her hall and crossed the rainbow bridge as she left the abode of the gods; she was all alone and on foot, and thought that all still slept. Unbeknown to the goddess, however, Loki noticed her movement, and, his curiosity piqued, he followed her as silently as a shadow. Freyja travelled all day across a rocky plain and frozen river and alongside a great glacier until, near nightfall, she followed the sound of hammering down a narrow passage and through a dank cavern into the hidden underground workshop of the dwarfs Álfrigg, Berlíngr, Dvalin and Grér. The goddess was at first blinded by the brilliant glare of the smithy until her gaze fell upon the most beautiful necklace she had ever seen, a river of precious fluid metal, and her heart was struck with an insurmountable desire to possess this peerless treasure. She offered the smiths gold and silver in great mounds, but the dwarfs refused with disdain what they had themselves already in plenty; only the price of her beautiful, shining body, to be shared in turn for a full night each, would satisfy the desire of the dwarfs, whose inflamed lust for the goddess reflected Freyja's own covetous longing for the necklace. Horrified by this demand, Freyja noticed for the first time the dark and ugly features of the misshapen dwarfs; her disgust, however, was soon outweighed by her desire, reckoning as she did that four nights in the foul embraces of the dwarfs was little enough to pay to be clasped for an eternity within the circlet of the most beautiful of treasures. Soon the deal was struck, and soon enough the bargain fulfilled: four nights later, the dwarfs fixed the necklace upon the goddess, and she departed, alone and undetected – or so she thought.

As Freyja entered the chambers of Sessrúmnir well-pleased with her new treasure, Loki, unseen by the goddess, continued on to the hall of the All-father, where he was all too happy to inform Odin that the object of the lust of the one-eyed god had sold herself to foul and repugnant dwarfs for the price of a bauble. Loki's mischievous joy turned quickly to cold fear in the face of the rage of Odin, however, who cast the trickster from his hall with the command that

Loki return with Freyja's ill-gotten treasure or not at all. The hall of Freyja is thought to be impassable to uninvited guests, but Loki was desperately afraid of the wrath of Odin, and so, taking on the shape of a fly, the Sly One searched high and low until he found a crack just big enough for a creepy-crawly insect to worm itself through. Once inside the hall, Loki silently found his way to the chamber of the goddess, who, like all her household, was fast asleep. Loki reached to take the necklace, but Freyja slept so that the clasp was covered. Transforming himself into the semblance of a flea, the trickster flitted about the body of the goddess, amusing himself upon her snowy terrain of flesh, and finally settling upon her cheek; finding a tender spot, the flea pierced Freyja's lovely skin. With a moan, the goddess turned in her sleep, exposing the clasp, and Loki, returned to his own form, soon pilfered the treasure with nimble fingers and fled Freyja's hall upon silent feet. When the goddess woke, she discovered her loss with a horror that soon turned to rage: only Loki might perform such a bold and audacious theft, and even he would be too timid without the express command of the Father of the Gods. Freyja stormed into Odin's presence to demand an apology, only to be confronted by his knowledge of her own whoring disgrace with the four dwarfs. The price of her necklace, Odin informed Freyja, was to be a recurring cycle of strife, bloodshed and magical resurrection through the dark forces of *seid*. The All-father commanded that Freyja bring two earthly rulers to the battlefield, each with twenty sub-kings and their warriors; as the armies slaughtered one another, the goddess was to devise incantations so that each bloody corpse might be brought back to life to fight again. Having sold her own body to gain her necklace, Freyja thought little of bartering the lives and bodies of warriors to regain the treasure, and so she and Odin reached an accord.

Necklaces have been associated with fertility goddesses in the Mediterranean from very early times, and there is evidence that this relationship also existed in southern Scandinavia from at least as early as the Bronze Age, as figures so adorned survive in Denmark dating from that period. Necklaces are generally thought to be vaginal symbols much like rings, and the Old Norse term *men* might be rendered as 'necklace' or 'girdle', either of which one might very well expect to be associated with fertility; indeed, it has been suggested that the key significance of this myth lies in its function as a study of the association between sexual promiscuity and the development of fertility. In this case, the goddess's acquisition of the necklace illustrates not only a facet of her character but both an adolescent coming-of-age narrative and a metaphor for the reawakening of fecundity with the coming of each new spring. Because of an analogous reference in *Beowulf*, *Brísinga* is generally assumed to refer to a lost family name; more provocatively, it is possible that the term is derived from *brísingr*, an uncommon Old Norse term for fire. *Brísingamen*, the 'necklace of fire', might then refer literally to the brightness of the treasure itself; moreover, it would be tempting in that case to wonder if the name also might connote metaphorically the burning lust so commonly associated with the goddess Freyja. It has also been suggested that such 'fire' refers to the sun, which clearly resonates with the function of Freyja as a fertility goddess. Regardless, it is clear that we find in the myth of Freyja's acquisition of her necklace an intriguing inversion of the myth of Frey's loss of his sword, which he traded for a chance to wed the giantess Gerd, with whom he was besotted: in both cases hidden desires lead goddess and god to act upon the basest of motivations in response to secret and transgressive glimpses of forbidden fruit, and in both cases physical objects are imbued with nearly palpable symbolism through their association with various incarnations of desire.

This myth also serves as a primer of sorts into several facets of the character of Loki, the most enigmatic figure of the Norse pantheon. The catalyst for Odin's reaction to Freyja's whoring is, after all, Loki's predisposition to spy and to tattle, nasty attributes which are fundamental aspects of his role as a troublemaker who brews dissension for the sheer joy of mischief. When he finds that the fire he has built to cook Freyja's goose threatens to scorch him, Loki saves himself with his skills as a shape-shifter and a thief. All of these characteristics emphasize Loki's demonic volatility. This myth also illustrates that Freyja herself is a complex deity, and comprises contending and paradoxical attributes: the easy virtue which submits to the demands of the lustful dwarfs elucidates Freyja's function as a fertility goddess, of course, but she acquiesces with equal equanimity to Odin's command to sow carnage and death, much as a Valkyrie does. This duality reflects the twin powers of fertility and destruction associated with Freyja, just as it reflects a similar duality concerning the forbidden magic she practised; it is thus noteworthy that Freyja has been convincingly linked with the figure of the sorceress thrice burned by the Æsir and thrice reborn through the flames. Thus began the first of all wars, in which *seid*, it should be remembered, was the great weapon of the fertility gods.

It is doubtless in any case that in Freyja we find the powers of life and death inextricably bound together; indeed, the terms Odin demands for the return of Freyja's necklace, a bargain which requires a continuing cycle of slaughter that is fed by miraculous resurrection, recalls both the spearing of and triple immolation of Gullveig, as recounted in the *Völuspá*, and reinforces Freyja's double identity. The rejuvenation of dead warriors in this myth echoes the daily battles of the *einherjar*, the dead warriors brought to Odin by the Valkyries to swell the ranks of the Æsir, and, perhaps tellingly, is also reminiscent of the warriors resurrected in the Cauldron of Plenty in the Welsh *Mabinogion*. In any case, this recurring battle is only ended, we are told in the late version of the story recorded in the Icelandic *Flateyjarbók*, through Christian intervention. This cycle of combat, referred to as Hjadningavíg, or the 'Strife of Hedin's men' after one of the two contending kings, thus provides a dark and gloomy counterpoint to the daily battles of Odin's heroes of Valhalla, who themselves, we know from our knowledge of the coming doom of Ragnarök, struggle in vain. Indeed, the motivations of the gods involved in this myth underscore their given functions and identities: Odin's jealous pride and seemingly needless bloodlust highlight and are highlighted by his need to swell the ranks of his warriors, as well as his nature as a war god; Loki's scheming prying and self-serving thieving illustrate his outsider status and his demonic nature as an enemy within the ranks of the gods; most importantly, Freyja's greedy materialism and overt and unapologetic sexuality bring to the fore the attributes and appetites to be associated with an ancient fertility goddess, while her association with death and dying elucidate her new and growing role as a destroyer goddess. Moreover, we can hardly attribute these characterizations as the work of the single hand of the author who recorded this myth; the sensibilities and actions resonate much too closely with the general characters of these gods as we know them.

Like her brother, Freyja is strongly linked with the boar, the association of which with both fecundity and ferocity mirrors the duality of the goddess herself. We learn in the eddic poem *Hyndluljód*, or *Lay of Hyndla*, that Freyja's familiar is Hildisvíni, 'Battle-swine', whose very name reflects the appetite of his mistress for slaughter. Freyja informs the giantess Hyndla that Hildisvíni is the creation of the dwarfs Dáin and Nabbi, and her description of her boar as glowing and golden-bristled offers a suggestive link to Frey's familiar Gullinbursti. Hyndla is not the first nor the last to accuse Freyja of wantonness, but it is significant that in this poem, the giantess points out that the battle-boar Freyja rides upon is in reality none other than Freyja's votary and lover Óttar the Simple, who has pleased his goddess with ample blood sacrifices, and whose disguise may echo the ritual use of boar masks in the cult of Freyja. The double entendre of the great *Syr*, or 'Sow', mounted upon her lover the Battle-Swine is hardly insignificant, and thus this amusing episode seemingly concerned primarily with the lineage of Óttar might also offer glimpses of various faces of the goddess and rites of her worship.

The goddess shows herself in a darker mask in the stories surrounding the fate of the most beautiful of the gods: Baldr, the brightest and most beloved of the gods, was slain at the hand of his blind brother Höd, who cast a seemingly harmless dart of mistletoe at his 'invulnerable' sibling, instigated and guided by the cunning and duplicity of the malicious trickster Loki. Baldr's wife, the goddess Nanna, was completely overcome with grief at the death of her beloved. In fact, her desolation was so complete that, as the gods settled Baldr among the grave goods atop the pyre on board the ship, Nanna's heart burst from grief, and so the Æsir set wife next to husband for the journey to Hel. The archetypal Dying God and his consort clearly seem to represent ancient fertility figures, and if Baldr is the sleeping seed planted within the grave of apparently desolate earth, Nanna is the dormant power of increase which languishes with that seed. Moreover, scholars have long suggested a link between this mythic episode and sati practices, or the ritual sacrifice of consorts at the funerals of powerful men. Sati is a specifically Indian practice, but scholars of Norse and Germanic literature have long noted similarities between sati and episodes like this one in Norse texts. Such similarities are all

the more provocative when one takes note of the ancient relationship between the Nordic and Indian mythologies. According to the
alternative version of the story of the death of the Baldr figure related
by Saxo, however, Nanna's beauty was a motive force behind the death
of Balderus, and thus in this iteration the ancient duality of the terrible beauty of the goddess is highlighted. In Saxo's account, Nanna
is a Norwegian princess who is married to Balderus's adversary and
killer Hotherus, who is cognate with the Höd of the more familiar
myth. In Saxo's version, it is jealousy concerning Nanna that leads
to the death of the Danish king Balderus, who is stabbed by a magic
sword (which pierces his invulnerability) by his rival.

In addition, tradition has long attempted to link the Norse Nanna
with her ancient Sumerian sister Inanna (also known as Nannar, or
Nana), known to the Babylonians as Ishtar. The Phrygian Attis was
the son of the eastern Nanna, whose consort was Baal, a figure from
the ancient Near East who has sometimes himself been linked with
Baldr. Although we must be extremely cautious in asserting that
these relationships prove a definitive link across thousands of miles
and years, the similarities of names and mythic archetypes certainly
are, on their faces, suggestive of the possibility of common echoes of
ancient fertility rites.

Our surmises concerning ritual sati practices in the northern
world are not confined to the myth of Baldr's funeral, however;
indeed, references to Scandinavian ship burials are not limited to
accounts from Norse and Anglo-Saxon literature. In fact, the most
vibrant and complete account is that of a Middle Eastern observer.
In the early tenth century, an Arab named Ahmad ibn Fadlan gave
an account of a ship burial among the Rus', or eastern Vikings; the
events he recounted took place along the banks of the Volga river. The
account of Ibn Fadlan is preserved in two sources: an eleventh-century
copy of the *Risala*, Ibn Fadlan's record of his travels, and the Persian
geographer Amin Razi's late sixteenth-century version of the same
text, which is thought to have been based on early manuscripts. This
account has some elements in common with the Old Norse mythic
description of Baldr's funeral, as well as with the ceremony described
at the end of the Old English epic *Beowulf*. Moreover, archaeological
excavations at sites such as Oseberg in Norway and Sutton Hoo in

The iconic Sutton Hoo helmet was wrought of iron and tinned copper-alloy with some silver inlay, gold and garnets; it was probably made in Sweden in the early 7th century and subsequently was deposited in the most famous ship burial in England. Its animal and warrior motifs hearken back to Odin and his Valkyries, although the very presence of such elaborate grave goods in a cenotaph – or empty tomb – also underscores the shifting mythologies and ritual practices of the Age of Conversion, as the battle goddess Valkyries became replaced by or transformed into Anglo-Saxon virgin warrior saints.

East Anglia, England, corroborate some details concerning the practice of sending significant persons on their voyage to the otherworld well endowed with valuable and useful goods. Ibn Fadlan relates that poor men were placed in small boats and burned without much ado, while rich men had their estates divided into thirds: one-third provided an inheritance for the family, one-third was spent on grave clothes and related goods, and one-third was dedicated to purchasing an intoxicating beverage with which the mourners drank themselves oblivious for the length of time it took to prepare the funeral, which in the particular case he describes was some ten days.

The body of the deceased was kept in a temporary grave until the ceremony was prepared, and according to this Arab observer, the corpse he saw was well preserved and little worse for the delay because of the cold of the country, except for the fact that the skin blackened from the frost. On the day of the funeral the body was exhumed, dressed in finery, placed on a pavilion on board a ship and surrounded by valuable goods, food and weapons. The ship itself had been placed on scaffolding that would serve as a great pyre. A number of animal sacrifices comprised an important aspect of the funeral: Ibn Fadlan mentions cows, a dog and hens. In addition to the description of the ship and pyre themselves, Ibn Fadlan's account of the sacrifice of a pair of horses is especially evocative of the story of Baldr's funeral. Furthermore, the theory of travel to the underworld, which is foundational to the ceremony recorded in this account, maintains that all the treasure, animals and persons consumed by the flames will be transported to the otherworld; indeed, a bystander commented to Ibn Fadlan upon the stiff wind fanning the blaze of the pyre – to this witness it seemed that the god wished his follower to join him all the sooner. After the ashes of the ship burial had cooled, our chronicler relates, the mourners erected a mound upon the spot. There are several references to funeral pyres in *Beowulf*, most notably the description of the hero's cremation at the very end of the epic. The *Beowulf* poet goes into more detail than Ibn Fadlan about the mound raised over the ashes of Beowulf and the treasure dedicated to him. We are told that the chosen spot was on a prominent headland, and that the walls were high and broad enough so that the tomb was visible from far out at sea; furthermore, the very best masonry work was dedicated to this monument.

According to Ibn Fadlan, an important aspect of the funeral ceremony he witnessed, for an important male personage, was the sacrifice of a female slave who volunteered to become her master's wife in death. Upon the occasion of the master's death, the female slaves were assembled and given the opportunity to join the dead man in a sort of posthumous marriage. One of the slave girls volunteered, and we are told that seldom had a victim to be compelled; Ibn Fadlan further notes that once the commitment was made, it could not be broken. For the time remaining until the funeral, the slave girl was bedecked in finery, sang and danced, drank her fill of the intoxicating beverage and performed ritual sex acts with the male kinsmen of her master (this the kinsmen did, so they claimed, out of loyalty and obligation to her lord). As the time for the ceremony approached, a ritual doorframe was erected, and the slave girl was hoisted to look over this frame to see into the next world. She was lifted three times: the first time she reported seeing her parents, the second time she claimed to see the host of her dead relations and the third time she cried out that she had seen her master awaiting her in a verdant paradise. She thus called out to be taken to her master, and she was brought on board the ship, where an old woman called the Angel of Death orchestrated another series of ritual sex acts, culminating in the sacrifice of the willing slave girl by strangulation and stabbing; meanwhile, the men outside the ship raised such a clamour that a slave girl witnessing the ceremony could not hear the sounds on the ship, and therefore would not fear to join her own master when the time came.

In the context of this account, the story of Nanna's heart bursting with despair at Baldr's funeral and ultimately sharing her husband's pyre aboard *Hringhorni* is rendered more than a little troubling; what at first blush seems in the myth a poignant description of spousal grief takes on sinister undertones in light of the Arab emissary's description of the ritual rape and human sacrifice of a slave bride aboard a ship burial. The evidence of language is also suggestive on this point: the Valkyries are referred to at least once, in *Vǫluspá*, as the *nannas* of Odin, and thus it is possible that *nanna* could refer to a woman or dedicated servant in general and not just to a particular individual married to Baldr, an evocative linguistic possibility which might link Nanna's death with the ritual human sacrifice described by Ibn

Fadlan. Furthermore, the fact that the slave girl was simultaneously strangled and stabbed is suggestive of an identification with sacrificial rites associated with Odin, whose victims and votaries were often marked with a spear, and who is of course himself the Hanging God. While hardly evidence of a definitive relationship, the resonance between the two episodes in any case forces a thoughtful reader to cast a somewhat critical eye over the death of Nanna in the myth of Baldr's funeral. Certainly the sacrifice of Baldr's horse and harness echoes the ritual described by Ibn Fadlan, as does the description of grave goods and ship burning, and these parallels suggest that we must closely examine the possible relationships between aspects of these episodes. On the other hand, the death of Lit, an unfortunate dwarf who ran under Thor's feet during the funeral ceremony, and whom the thunder god kicked onto the pyre to burn, has no clear parallel. Although Lit is described in some sources as an enemy of the gods, it would be difficult to prove that his death represents a traditional funeral rite of some kind, although it has been suggested that his dying contortions might hearken back to funereal cultic dancing. As tempting as such a reading might be, we cannot substantiate such an assertion with any confidence, and thus, more than in the case of the description of the death of Nanna, Thor's slaying of the dwarf remains rather unintelligible; some might say that it takes on the trappings of a comic interlude. The burning of Baldr's ship, however, remains a deadly serious affair, serving as it does as a foretaste of the conflagration to come, that which concludes Ragnarök.

Any discussion of death in general, or The Doom of the Gods in particular, requires that we examine Hel, the death goddess of the northern world. Snorri describes Niflheim as an abode for the dead into which Odin cast Hel, the daughter of Loki, who thus became queen of the underworld. Hel is described as being half white and half black, half beautiful woman and half rotting corpse. An inversion of the Apples of Idun emphasizes this duality: just as those golden apples are the fruit of life, which offer eternal youth, so the Apples of Hel are linked with death in Norse poetry. Hel thus exemplifies another manifestation of the 'terrible beauty' of the northern goddess, wherein terror, death and destruction are often hand in glove with beauty, life and creation, and some have compared Hel to the

Indian goddess Kali in this respect. Hel holds sway over a realm below and to the north, a direction which offers a possible clue to ancient origins: *north* in the Germanic languages is related to the Greek term *nerteros*, 'regarding the nether-regions'. 'North' is generally taken as 'lower left' in the ancient Scandinavian languages, relative to one facing east and given the position of the noontime sun in the northern sky. Hel's domain is the home of those who die of disease and old age, and is described as a dank, dark, unpleasant place: Hel's hall is known as Eljudnir, 'Damp Spot', where her manservant is Ganglati, 'Slow One'; her maidservant is Ganglot, 'Lazy One'; Hel's bed is Kor, 'Sickness'; and her table is set with 'Hunger'.

Hel, whose name evokes the 'hidden', 'concealed' and 'secret' nature of the grave and thus of the nether regions in several Germanic languages, represents a late, perhaps Christian-era, personification of the underworld; a certain intensification of the concept of a dark and dismal afterlife into a place of 'hellish' torment might well have resulted through a Christian revision of the old myths. While the term 'Niflheim' seems to come from Snorri, the related name Niflhel, 'Dark Hell' or 'Misty Hell', appears to have been used earlier. Snorri uses these names almost interchangeably, however, and suggests that both these terms refer to the ninth world, a 'lower hell' (as an alternate reading of *nifl* might suggest) reserved for the truly evil dead. Muspell (or Muspelheim), the land of fire, is generally not counted among the nine worlds, but clearly was thought to have existed before the Creation and was expected to consume the world after the cataclysmic battle of Ragnarök. The pagan Germanic concept of a land of fire and its relationship with an apocalyptic end of the world survived the conversion to Christianity, and related terms and concepts reassert themselves in Old Saxon, Old High German and Old English religious literature. Hel – along with her bastard siblings Jörmundgandr, the World Serpent, and Fenrir, the great wolf who will swallow Odin in the final battle – was spawned by the demonic trickster Loki upon the loins of the giantess Angrboda, 'Grief-bringer', and all three of these siblings represent the forces of evil, chaos and destruction that the Scandinavian gods try, ultimately in vain, to keep at bay.

This 6th-century Merovingian bird brooch calls to mind the associations between various Celtic goddesses and birds.

V

The Seductive Destruction of the Goddess of the Western Isles

Genesis

When we speak of the ancient cultural ancestors of the British and the Irish, we generally refer to the Celts. Beginning with ancient Greek commentators four or five centuries before the birth of Christ, we are offered glimpses into the lives of a people who moved from east to west until the *Keltoi* had occupied a broad swathe of western Europe north of the Alps. The Celts themselves were illiterate until their contact with the classical world, so most of what we know about them is refracted through a Mediterranean lens. Luckily, however, the material objects they left behind allow archaeologists today to give compelling voice to the culture of these people, who seemed to have made great strides in weaponry and riding tack as they shifted readily from Bronze to Iron during what archaeologists call the Hallstatt period around 800 BCE.

Hallstatt is the name of a great cemetery of the era in modern Austria, and the objects found there give evocative evidence of the rise of a rich and widespread Celtic culture. Within a few centuries, a later phase of Celtic development, referred to as La Tène, associated with Lake Neuchâtel in Switzerland, testifies to the ascendancy of a warrior elite, which rode to battle on lightweight, iron-wheeled chariots. Eventually the Roman Empire stemmed the Celtic tide, and by the beginning of the Common Era the Gauls, as the Celts were known to the Romans, had been subjugated, as Caesar so famously recorded in his *Gallic Wars*. By the middle of the first century CE most of the isle of Britain south of Scotland was firmly under Roman control as well, although Ireland never fell under the direct sway of the empire. The Romans left the British Isles in the mid-fifth

This copper-alloy Celtic mother goddess figure dates from 3rd-century Roman Britain and was excavated as part of the Southbroom Hoard in Wiltshire. It was part of a set of gods and goddesses.

century CE, and soon thereafter an influx of Germanic invaders known as the Saxons, the Angles and the Jutes would establish England, the land of the Angles.

All of Britain and Ireland eventually fell under the political and cultural dominance of the English, although around the year 500 a great Welsh leader bought a short respite at the Battle of Badon, and the ensuing generation or so which followed offers in rosy hindsight the golden age of King Arthur. Although the term 'Celtic' is thrown around today with more fervour than accuracy, it is undoubtedly true that medieval Irish and Welsh literary traditions contain more than a few ancient Celtic elements; as we may discern a far-off Romanized Briton in the legends of Arthur, we may catch an occasional glimpse of the face of the Celtic goddess in the tales of her medieval Irish and Welsh children.

Medieval literary material which displays aspects of the visage of the ancient Celtic goddess is preserved in both Irish and Welsh sources, with the Irish tradition broken into four main cycles. The mythological cycle includes the *Dindshenchas* (History of Places), and much more notably the *Lebor Gabála Érenn* (The Book of the Taking of Ireland, or Book of Invasions), which includes much of what we know about the Celtic pantheon, especially as elucidated in descriptions of the Tuatha Dé Danann, the 'Tribe of the Goddess Danu'. The Fenian Cycle tells of the heroics of Finn MacCool (Fionn mac Cumaill) and his band of followers, known as the Fianna or Fenians; the Cycle of Kings purports to be a historical record of the early kings of Ireland; and the Ulster Cycle includes the *Táin Bó Cúailnge*, the 'Cattle Raid of Cooley', at the centre of which is the great Irish hero Cúchculainn, who comes into contact and conflict with potent female figures such as Queen Medb and the Morrígan, two clear avatars of the ancient Celtic goddess. The Ulster Cycle is preserved in two manuscripts, one from the twelfth and one from the late fourteenth century – the oral sources for these texts seem to have been much earlier, however, and thus elements of the stories reach back into the misty past. The Welsh tradition is best preserved within the compilation known as the *Mabinogion*, which may be broken into four main branches, in addition to four independent Welsh tales and three later Arthurian romances. The *Mabinogion* is also recorded in two manuscripts, one from the early fourteenth century and one

This sword, found in Britain and dating from the period 200–100 BCE, illustrates key aspects of the Iron Age Celtic La Tène culture.

about a hundred years younger, although again, much of the source material seems to be far older.

Although some of the Irish and Welsh stories of warriors and adventures which survive from the Middle Ages may at first glance seem to have little to tell us about the nature of the goddess, the careful reader will perceive her face emerging again and again in the guise of strong and independent female figures. The Celtic goddess of old is perhaps most readily apparent in the form of Irish queens and battle Furies who are fierce opponents as well as ardent lovers, who thus embody powers of life-giving and life-taking in equal measure, and who – once spurned – are tireless and remorseless in their search for vengeance. Their Welsh sisters, on the other hand, are often figures of potent magic who recast roles of the ancient goddess in the trappings of medieval folklore and romance.

Faces of the Goddess

The Irish mother goddess Ana or Anu, 'Abundance' (sometimes given as Danu), is the eponymous matron of the Tuatha Dé Danann, the group of Irish gods named for their lineage as the descendants of the goddess Ana. Primarily a fertility goddess, Ana is associated with the prosperity of Ireland, which in medieval verse is often rendered Iath n'Annan, the 'Land of Ana'. This goddess is often associated very closely with the fecundity of Munster in particular, and the name Dá Chích Anann, usually rendered 'Paps of Anu' (referring to the breasts of the goddess) is the name given to two rounded hills in County Kerry near Killarney. Like many of her Indo-European sisters we have met thus far, and indeed, as with great goddesses throughout the world, Ana comprised both productive and destructive forces – some see the war goddess the Morrígan as one of the many faces of Ana – especially as these are outgrowths of the potent powers of love, lust and lineage. The traditional Irish notion of a rightful king as the consort of a goddess who embodies her nation may stem from the fact that these dual aspects of the goddess as nurturer and protector represent vital attributes of a successful reign.

Others have linked this fertility figure with Áine, a fairy embodiment of lust and carnality who is sometimes seen as a woman stolen from the mortal world on account of her ravishing beauty; in any case, a salient link to the identity of Ana is the fact that Áine is claimed by various prominent families as an ancestor. Another provocative possibility is a connection between the goddess Ana and the medieval Irish saint of the same name. Many have argued that Danu or Dana is the Gaulish form of the deity commonly known as Ana in Ireland, and cite as evidence for this position place names such as Danube, a form which seems to refer to such a goddess in various languages. Moreover, Danu is the name of a significant goddess in several eastern Indo-European traditions, perhaps most notably in the Indian Rig Veda, in which this figure is associated with the cosmic powers of water. Although Ana/Anu and Danu/Dana are traditionally accepted as variant medieval Irish forms ultimately representing the same (or closely related) ancient Celtic figure(s), this assessment is rejected by some, most usually on linguistic grounds. The circumstantial similarities are seductive, however, and certainly compelling enough to warrant closer examination. It is therefore of special interest that the Welsh mother goddess bears a similar name.

The Welsh female deity Dôn, not to be confused with the Irish male figure Donn, is generally accepted as the medieval British incarnation of the ancient Celtic mother goddess thought to survive in Gaul as Danu and in Ireland as Ana, although some dispute this connection. Dôn may have been associated with powers of fertility and is usually thought to be the consort of Beli. Most of what we know about Dôn we glean from the fourth branch of the *Mabinogion*, in which she is identified as the sister of Math fab Mathonwy and as the mother of at least one girl, Arianrhod, and three sons, Gilfaethwy, Gwydion and Gofannon. In *Culhwch and Olwen* we learn that Dôn also had a fourth son by the name of Amaethon. Some sources suggest that she had several more children, most manifesting divine attributes; thus Arianrhod may be a reflection of an ancient dawn goddess, Gofannon is cast in the image of a smith god of old, and so forth. In this way, Dôn would function as the mother of the gods in much the same way as her Irish sister Ana gave birth to the Tuatha Dé Danann. These children of Dôn, or the forces of light and goodness, are often seen as opposing the children of Llŷr, or the powers of dark and evil. Moreover, Dôn seems to have given birth to life-giving waters, and just as Danu and Ana are often associated with watercourses, it has been argued that rivers throughout the Celtic world designated with the elements Dôn or Donwy take their names from this goddess, as does the constellation Cassiopeia, which is called Llys Don, the 'Retinue of Dôn', in Welsh. As an interesting side note, some confusion in the medieval period results in Dôn being conflated at times with a Christian saint, Anne.

The Great Mother was widely worshipped throughout the Celtic world, and this veneration is attested in well over a thousand extant inscriptions and religious statues. The goddess is most commonly found represented in triple forms known as Deae Matres, always in the plural, which are usually found in the vicinity of ritual precincts. These figures were clearly fertility icons, and are usually represented holding the bounty of the harvest, including fruits and loaves, as well as babies; sometimes these figures are baring a breast. The hair and head-coverings of the images indicate that both matrons and maidens are represented, and it is possible that, in addition to their obvious function as fertility goddesses, these triplet statues indicate the three stages of the role of women in Celtic society: virgin, wife and crone. The latent and manifest fertility of the first two functions is counterbalanced by the crone's role in laying out the dead, which may suggest the nurturing and destructive faces of the Great Goddess herself. This duality is manifested in the fact that Deae Matres fertility figurines have been linked to goddesses as disparate as Epona and the Morrígan.

A variation of the Deae Matres are the Deae Nutrices; these mother goddesses illustrate their roles as nurturers and healers through the image of the goddess suckling a child. Such goddesses are sometimes rendered as a single figure, which is therefore referred to as a Dea Nutrix. Deae Nutrices are sometimes associated with centres of healing rituals. Matrona is the name given to the ancient Gaulish mother goddess associated with the river Marne in France, and especially with a sanctuary near its source. Many sets of triple Matronae have been found, and these are especially common in the valley of the Rhine. Modron is commonly accepted as the medieval Welsh manifestation of Matrona. Modron is the mother of Mabon, the kidnapped boy in *Culhwch and Olwen* who embodies the ancient

This 6th- or 7th-century pendant bowl displays the abiding influence of Celtic art during the period of the Anglo-Saxon conquest of England.

myth of the child abducted from the great goddess of fertility by the powers of the underworld; this theft of fertility by sterility represents the endless struggle between the forces of life and those of death. Modron is transformed in the Arthurian tradition into the strong, potent woman Morgan le Fay. Mabon resurfaces also in the tales of Arthur; moreover, it is assumed by many that Mabon, 'Youth', is himself the erstwhile eponymous hero of the *Mabinogion*, and is therefore associated with Pryderi. Mabon is widely accepted to be derived from Maponos, 'Divine Young Man', a god of Celtic Britain.

A phenomenon related to that of the Three Mothers is the presence of the demigods Genii Cucullati, Latin for 'Hooded Fertility Spirits', generally rendered as small dwarf-like figures draped in the *cucullatus*, a distinctive Gaulish hooded cloak generally fastened shut from shoulder to knee. Devotees of the cults of these spirits are thought to have worn such cloaks themselves. Dating from the period of Roman sovereignty over the Celtic world, such figurines often appear in shrines associated with the Three Mothers or other fertility figures, notably the divine pair of Rosmerta and Mars in Britain. Genii Cucullati sometimes seem to be making a sacrifice to or receiving a gift from the mother goddess; more often they appear holding eggs in obvious reference to powers of fertility, and they are sometimes depicted with scrolls or swords, the latter of which emphasize the phallic function of fecundity attributed to these consorts of the mother goddess. In a number of cases, such symbolism is more blatant: some such images, when the hoods are removed, are little more than huge erect phalli, while in other cases the phallus of a Genius Cucullatus may be utilized as a lamp-holder. The analysis of some scholars could be thought to suggest that still other figurines emphasize the ambiguous sexuality and even hermaphroditic attributes associated with some fertility cults. According to such interpretations, these images offer the suggestion of rounded breasts beneath their cloaks, and perhaps feminine facial features. Genii Cucullati were commonly associated with sacred wells and springs in ancient Britain and sometimes in Gaul as well, reinforcing their association with the life-giving power of these water sources in general and with the mother goddesses venerated at these shrines in particular. These shrines were very often thought to have potent healing powers, and thus the Genii Cucullati may be thought to evoke the restorative, as well as the generative, powers of fertility deities.

In stark contrast to the most common depictions of dwarfs in the Germanic mythology of their Northern neighbours, therefore, the Genii Cucullati depicted in Celtic shrines are associated with life force, fertility and healing. Some have argued, however, that the hooded nature of these forms suggests that they may also serve as guides to the otherworld. Although at times a Genius Cucullatus appears as a single figure, Genii Cucullati usually appear in triplicate, at least in Britain. This pattern of tri-form images not only strengthens the association between the Genii Cucullati and the Deae Matres, but underscores a fundamental theme of Celtic mythology in general: the multiplication of figures, as well as the enlargement of features and the addition of attributes, such as horns, are all ways of expressing the supernatural intensity of the powers of generation and restoration inherent in fertility figures. It is important to note that this theme is also symbolized by the common Central European Genius Cucullatus, which, although appearing in single form, often is represented as a lone giant rather than as three dwarfs. An outsized figure represents the same intensification principle as tripled images. Given the symbolism inherent in the size and number of the depicted images, it is perhaps not surprising that some representations of Genii Cucullati are highly stylized and at times somewhat abstract, in general emphasizing the tripartite nature of these figures, as well as their eponymous and emblematic cloaks, to the detriment of realist depiction. Some have argued that such abstract representation emphasizes a general trend towards fundamental and intentional ambiguity in Celtic religious symbols, which thus might be all the more subject to personal interpretation through their very open-endedness. There is a dearth of direct literary evidence relating to the Genii Cucullati, and thus it is difficult to assess precisely the relevance of these antique Celtic figures to medieval Irish and Welsh mythology. It is perhaps in their triplism, in their relationship as consorts to mother goddesses, and in their clear manifestation of fertility motifs that they speak most eloquently to recurring mythological themes in the literary traditions of the Middle Ages.

One of the most well-known and widespread faces of the Celtic goddess was that of the equine deity Epona. Horses played vital roles in Celtic culture from the very earliest appearances of these peoples upon the stage of history, and equine images and the animals they represented were significant in rituals, cults and related artefacts from at least the Bronze Age. Horses were vital for their labour, revered for their military use as well as for the social status their possession conferred, and venerated as symbols of both agricultural fecundity and sexual prowess. It should come as no surprise, then, that, judging from the extant material record, Epona, the 'Divine Horse-mistress', was among the most popular of the Celtic deities; her worship spread from its original home in eastern Gaul to cover the entire Roman Empire from the Balkans to Iberia, from the very epicentre of the empire at Rome itself to the extreme frontier outpost of the British Isles, having been imported to both locales by Roman cavalrymen. Epona's name refers to her primary function as the patroness of horses, a role which seems also to have included draft animals such as mules and donkeys. Originally a primarily rural deity often venerated in shrines in stables, over time her worship spread, and eventually she was inducted into the Roman collection of gods, with a day – 18 December – dedicated to her. Approximately sixty named inscriptions to the Horse Mistress survive, in addition to perhaps four times that many in graphic images.

Epona is generally depicted as a female figure riding side-saddle, although sometimes she is seated upon a throne between a number of horses; very often she holds fruit or other symbols of fertility and plenty. Other animals associated with Epona through iconography include dogs, foals, small birds and giant horned geese, upon which the goddess is occasionally depicted as a passenger. The Divine Rider is inextricably linked with the horse, her eponymous symbol, and we are hard pressed to find examples of renderings of the deity which do not include representations of horses. Images depicting the goddess are numerous and widespread, spanning the whole of the Celtic world; the recurring attributes of the Horse Goddess allow us to identify these images with reasonable certainty, in spite of the fact that only a relative handful of them are inscribed with her name. Although traditional scholarship linked Epona with the great chalk horse at Uffington, more recent studies have called this association into question. Epona was the goddess of horse-breeding and of cavalrymen and their mounts, and in this function she was adopted by many Roman legionnaires; indeed, she is the only purely Celtic goddess we know with certainty was worshipped in Rome itself. Moreover, Celtic deities generally are firmly rooted in the landscape, its features and its powers of fecundity and production, and the Horse Goddess is no exception. She is also a goddess of fertility and of plenty, and she may in some instances be related to healing cults. Indeed, Epona has something of an association with thermal springs, sometimes appearing naked and almost nymph-like in aspect; in addition, in a few places she might be linked to sun worship, both through her totemic horse, an animal often associated with sun cults, and perhaps through her relationship to a male consort solar deity. Epona in her guise as fertility goddess is closely associated with the tradition of the Deae Matres, and in fact appears in at least one significant depiction in tripartite form, in which the triple 'Horse Goddesses' are known as Eponabus.

Some scholars believe that a female horse deity is a natural manifestation of the vital role women played in agriculture and in the rearing of animals; according to this line of argument, the later appropriation of this goddess by a warrior cult of cavalrymen would serve to obscure this original function. In the context of her relationship with graves and cemeteries, it has been suggested that Epona might also have comprised some chthonic functions, perhaps as a guide to the underworld. Vestiges of the ancient Gaulish deity Epona are often attributed to her medieval Welsh relation Rhiannon, both through associations with horses and with plenty; moreover, many see a resemblance to Epona in her medieval Irish kinswoman Macha, who, as an embodiment of sovereignty and as a war goddess associated with horses, also unites Epona's combination of the forces of fertility and destruction, as well as manifesting a relationship with the Gaulish goddess's signature animal.

In opposition to, or perhaps as an aspect of, the Three Mothers of Celtic mythology, the Morrígna (the plural form of Morrígan), are the 'Great Queens' of the Irish battlefield. Triplism played a significant role in Celtic mythology, although how exactly these tripartite forms are to be divided and understood is by no means clear. The three war goddesses of the medieval Irish pantheon are sometimes said to be Badb, Macha and the Morrígan, but there are, on the other hand, no fewer than three distinct Machas, and some would posit that many of these various figures are in fact merely reflections of the same Morrígan, who may in turn be, in simplest terms, the destructive visage of the productive Great Mother. It would be obtuse to ignore the resonance between the Irish Furies and their Indo-European cousins, most especially in the form of the Norse Valkyries, who also sometimes appear in threes, who likewise delight in martial slaughter and destruction, and who also often take both a close interest in a particular hero and are associated with his demise. Unlike the generally virginal Valkyries, however, the Morrígna are overtly sexual and promiscuous, usually favouring their lovers in battle and taking special pleasure in pursuing and observing the demise of those who have scorned their advances. The duality of the powers of life and death inherent in the goddess is manifested through the insatiable twin appetites of the Morrígna, who embody both the carnal desire associated with the conception of life and the bloodlust which revels in violent death.

Moreover, although the Valkyries themselves often take the form of swans, they are associated with the raven through their lord Odin. Carrion birds, such as crows and ravens, were commonly associated with battle and death in northwest Europe, of course, and so the fact that Celtic and Germanic battle goddesses were so closely related to these birds may be coincidental, but given the long-standing resonance between these two strains of Furies, reaching far back into the Indo-European past, it is in any case a coincidence worth noting. Badb, the 'Hooded Crow' goddess, also known as Badb Catha, 'Battle Crow', is a Valkyrie-like medieval Irish denizen of the battleground closely associated with these carrion birds, and may be descended from an ancient Celtic deity called Bodua or Catu Bodua, Gaulish names cognate with Badb's own. Though sometimes rendered as a bloodthirsty mortal woman endowed with second sight and magical powers, this Irish fury seems to have descended from a long line of Indo-European war goddesses who claimed the spoils of battle carnage in a wide swathe from India to Iceland. Badb herself appears before Cúchulainn as a battle goddess, driving a chariot and bathed in blood, complete with red mantle and crimson eyebrows. Indeed, it is in the Ulster Cycle that Badb manifests most fully as a battle fury, wreaking havoc and sowing panic through her presence and appearance rather than through force of arms and direct action. The terror and mayhem she incites, especially in the men of Connacht, reflects both her role as a battle goddess and her function as an oracle of destruction – to see this goddess at all can be tantamount to a death blow. Hearing her call in the night, so the *Táin* tells us, one hundred men were struck down by fear, never to see the dawn. In *Da Derga's Hostel* she appears to King Conaire in tripartite form as three shrivelled black crones, more akin to crows than women, filthy and covered in crusted blood with loops of rope around their necks; Conaire is marked for death by this apparition, the nooses of which perhaps reflect ancient sacrificial rites. It is perhaps no surprise, then, that in subsequent traditions this goddess transforms

This 6th-century Merovingian bird brooch evokes the haunting image of the Badhbh Chaointe, the 'Keening Crow', a medieval Irish handmaid of battle and slaughter.

into a shadowy harbinger of doom known as the Badhbh Chaointe, the 'Keening Crow', a banshee-like figure sometimes glimpsed in the environs of bloody conflict. Though she often takes the form of a Cailleach, an 'old crone' or hag, Badb also may transform herself into an enchanting and alluring young woman; the sexual tension inherent in a trope involving such a powerful figure which may transform itself from nubile beauty into loathsome hag at will or whim touches upon a test that is related to the sovereignty theme, a commonplace of medieval Irish mythology in which a ruler valid-ates his kingship by communing with a goddess. A related theme survives in Geoffrey Chaucer's 'The Wife of Bath's Tale', as well as in the 'Loathly Lady' theme of several medieval romances. It is, how-ever, with the shape of the crow that this battle fury is most readily identified. In medieval Irish literature, it is Badb who guarantees victory to the Dagda before the Second Battle of Mag Tuired, and she appears in her signature form of a crow in her attempt to terrify the great hero of the Irish epics Cúchulainn. It is this bird that gives the goddess her name, of course, and the iconography of the crow or raven has a long lineage in Celtic culture; ancient Celtic coins conflated images of crows and horses to evoke such a goddess, and other coins, depicting nude female figures brandishing swords in an orgy of battle lust, reinforce this association. Ravens and crows appear in many contexts in Celtic art, usually evoking the underworld or foretelling doom, twin functions which were conjoined in Druidic fortune-telling rituals involving ravens.

Although several figures bearing the name Macha appear in different tales and perform various functions in medieval Irish mythology, the three main entities by that name provide us yet again with an example of the tripartite goddess. Some suggest that, in the first visage, as the queen of the ruler of Scythian invaders of Ireland, Macha displays attributes of a fertility goddess and aspects of sovereignty. This Macha was the wife of Nemed, king of the third great wave attempting to conquer Ireland, an influx of a people known as Nemedians, whose deeds are recounted in the *Book of Invasions*. Macha is said in this source to have died after twelve years as queen, and this version tells relatively little about her; still, her role as queen, especially in the context of a fertile plain dedicated to her by Nemed, suggests that she may have acted in the capacity of a divine consort who validates and blesses her king's reign. This Macha foretells the doom that will be wrought by the events recounted in the *Táin*, just as another Macha pronounces the curse which debilitates the Ulstermen during those events. In this first iteration of her story, Emain Macha and Ard Macha, rendered 'Armagh' in modern Ireland, are named after Macha, the latter because she is said to have been buried there. In a second visage, the fecundity and fleetness of foot of the Macha who lends her name to the capital of Ulster and her curse to its heroes has often caused her to be seen as a manifestation of the Horse Goddess. Indeed, as the wife of the mortal Cruinniuc (or Crunnchu), Macha combines fertile loins and horse-like swiftness in a way that both recalls the Gaulish Epona and links this Irish figure with her Welsh cousin Rhiannon.

Appearing mysteriously at the house of Cruinniuc one day, Macha began to keep house for the farmer; before nightfall she circled his threshold thrice, turning 'sunwise', or to the right, in a ritual enacted to evoke prosperity and good luck. Upon completion of this rite, Macha entered the bed of Cruinniuc, which she likewise blessed with a fertility soon manifested in her conception of twins. Cruinniuc's farm, already successful, soon burst at the seams with an agricultural plenty that accompanied the burgeoning body of Macha. As her delivery day approached, however, Cruinniuc determined to attend a gathering of all the Ulstermen at the court of King Conchobar mac Nessa; although his wife advised him not to go, Cruinniuc was adamant, and so Macha pleaded with him at the very least not to mention her or her powers. Like most foolish mortals with supernatural wives, however, Cruinniuc was unable to follow the wise advice of his wife, and through this foolishness, he lost her. It so happened that, while watching the royal chariots race, Cruinniuc exclaimed that his wife could outpace the king's tired nags; outraged and humiliated by this boast, Conchobar commanded the poor wretch to prove his words on the spot or to forfeit his life for his idle boast. Commanding Cruinniuc to be seized, the king sent for Macha, who, upon her arrival, was ordered to race the horses or to watch her husband die for his foolishness. Although she pleaded for mercy due to her condition, and asked for a delay until after the impending birth of her children, Conchobar proved as foolish as Cruinniuc, much to the distress of subsequent generations of Ulstermen. Indeed, in this version of Macha's story we are told that even the name of the capital of Ulster itself, Emain Macha, the 'Twins of Macha', memorializes this event and its dire consequences, supposedly because here Macha in her guise as the wife of Cruinniuc was forced, at the apex of her pregnancy, to race the swiftest of the king's horses, thereby causing the onset of labour. Macha won the race, thereby proving Cruinniuc's boast and saving his life, but at a great cost to herself and all of Ulster. Dying in painful childbirth to give birth to the twins, after whom the location of her torment henceforth would be known, with her final breath Macha pronounced a great curse upon the Ulstermen: for nine generations, all those men within hearing distance of her screams of torment, and all those descended from those witnesses, would be struck down, at the hour of their greatest need, with the *noínden* (birth pangs), a pain akin to that of Macha's in childbirth, which would last for five days and four nights. The sufferers would be, during this period, as weak and vulnerable as a woman giving birth. Only women, beardless boys and Cúchulainn himself were exempted from this curse. Macha's speed and association with horses in this story provides an obvious link with the Horse Goddess tradition, and her fertility of body and the agricultural fecundity which she brings to the fields of Cruinniuc reflect her lineage as a fertility goddess. Moreover, other sources suggest that a ceremony dedicated to the goddess Macha was held on Samain in order to keep the powers of the Otherworld, most virulent in this world during that time, at bay. Ritual horse racing is said to have formed a major component of that festival.

In addition, Macha's bountiful union to a mortal in this version reminds us of the sovereignty theme, especially in the context of this Macha's interaction with the royal court, which is a skewed reflection of the proper relationship between a mortal ruler and the embodiment of succour and stability. The curse which Macha pronounces upon a cruel and immoderate king provides an inversion of the sovereignty theme, and illuminates the destructive powers of the protector goddess. Just as a rightful king ensures fertility and protection through his communion with a divine consort, a foolish king alienates his people from this bounty and security, inflicting them with the sterility of all the suffering of childbirth while denying them the fertile fruits of this labour, and condemning them to this fate at the precise moment when strength is most needed to protect the kingdom.

Macha's third visage, in a narrative which provides the most information for this figure in medieval Irish mythology, is one that clearly reveals her identity as a manifestation of the Morrígna alongside Badb and the Morrígan. 'Macha's Harvest' is reaped through the decapitation of warriors, whose heads are the fruits of this labour; Macha has thus at times been equated with her Indo-European cousin Kali, the Destroyer, who appears ornamented with a necklace comprised of the skulls of the slain. In a euhemerized form, this goddess appears as the daughter of Áed Rúad, and is known as Macha Mong Ruad, 'Crimson-haired Macha'. The tale concerning Macha Mong Ruad certainly reflects aspects of the battle fury's appetite for slaughter and power over men, as well as her sexuality and her relationship to the sovereignty theme. Áed Rúad was one of three rival kings, all cousins, compelled under a *geis*, a sacred commitment or taboo, to share rule by turns of seven years each. After the death of Áed, his cousins denied his daughter the right to ascend to the throne because she was a woman. Macha soon came to power, however, when one rival was conveniently dispatched, many suggest at Macha's own hand; she also routed that competitor's sons in battle. She soon lured her other rival to her bed, married him and dominated him as his queen. Fearing that her hold on the throne was still not secure, she transformed herself into a leper and visited the surviving claimants to the throne who might contest her rule. Flirting with each in turn, she led them one by one into a nearby wood, promising to assuage the burning lust she incited in each one. In the cover of the forest she overcame and manacled each in his turn. Thus enslaving her remaining rivals, she forced them to build for her a mighty fort and capital to which she lent her name, according to the folk etymology offered by this version: she marked out the perimeter for the walls with a torc, *eo*, from her neck, *muin*, and hence the stronghold of Ulster was known as Emain Macha, the 'Neck-ring of Macha'. Such a torc must have been vast indeed, and seems to have come from the neck of a goddess to be both feared and desired. Indeed, Macha Mong Ruad evokes the ancient battle fury as well as the sovereignty theme, as she is a figure closely concerned with rightful rule, succession and blood feud; moreover, her martial prowess is combined with guile and an ability to use her femininity, maligned in her bid to ascend the throne, as a tool to subjugate the men who would dominate her politically as well as sexually. Likely descended from the ancient Celtic great goddess herself, these tripartite forms reveal aspects of a Macha who is both potent fertility figure and destructive battle fury, and her association with horses and with the Horse Goddess is further emphasized through her name's association with the steed of Cúchulainn, which is called Liath Macha, the 'Grey of Macha' – and its common appellation, the 'Battle-grey'. Finally, like her sister goddesses categorized as Morrígna, Macha may appear as a raven or a crow.

The archetypal battle fury of medieval Irish myth is the Morrígan, and many would posit that the other Morrígna are simply alternate

This torc, from the Ipswich Hoard of 1968–9, was excavated in England and dates to 150–50 BCE. It illustrates the personal ornamentation of the Iron Age Celtic La Tène culture.

faces of this particular war goddess. In a bloodthirsty rendition of the sovereignty theme, the sexually voracious Morrígan grants victory upon the battlefield to her lovers while attempting to hinder and destroy those who spurn her advances. In the most famous examples of the Morrígan's sexually charged and graphically depicted version of the sovereignty role, the Morrígan displays the opposite sides of the coin of her function as the ultimate femme fatale. In the first instance, in a prologue to the *Cath Maige Tuired*, we are informed that, during the festival of Samain one year, the Dagda came upon the Morrígan, who was washing herself with one foot on either bank of the River Unshin. The Dagda copulated with the Morrígan as she spanned the stream, thereby enacting, some maintain, an ancient fertility ritual. Thus having performed ritual coitus with the Dagda, the Morrígan promised her paramour aid on the battlefield and foretold the victory of the Tuatha Dé Danann over the Fomorians; according to at least one source, she then enacted a ritual sacrifice to ensure this victory, slaying the Fomorian warrior Indech and sharing out his blood by the handful to the waiting warriors summoned by the Dagda. The Morrígan, in any case, swore her loyalty to the Dagda's cause after their sexual union. In some sources the Morrígan is identified as the consort to the Dagda, perhaps suggesting that their ritual intercourse signified a longstanding arrangement more typical of the sovereignty theme.

In the second instance, during the course of the *Táin* the Morrígan appeared to the great hero of Ulster Cúchulainn in the form of a beautiful princess; she offered him her treasure, cattle, land and love. When the warrior remarked that a campaign was hardly a good time for romance, the lovely young woman suggested that she might offer her lover aid. Cúchulainn then coarsely rejected this offer, interpreting it as a brazen suggestion to couple with the princess. Enraged, the fury swore that she would hinder the hero in the form of an eel, in which guise she would trip him as he forded a stream; he responded that he would crack her eel ribs with his foot, maiming her forever unless he offered her his blessing. The Morrígan then swore that, in the form of a grey wolf-bitch, she would stampede animals against his crossing; Cúchulainn answered that he would put out her eye with a sling stone, disfiguring her forever unless he offered her his blessing. Finally, the war goddess swore that she would send stampeding cattle against him as he crossed the water by taking on the form of a red heifer; the hero replied that he would splinter her leg bone with a stone, laming her forever unless he offered her his blessing. Each foretold event came to pass, and the Morrígan was maimed, disfigured and lamed, leaving Cúchulainn victorious but wearied with his toil. The crafty fury then appeared to the hero in the form of a hideous hag milking a cow with three teats; she offered Cúchulainn a drink from each, and, refreshed more with each swallow, he offered her three blessings in return, thereby unknowingly lifting the wounds he had wrought upon her. When the hero realized that he had been fooled, he wished he could take back his blessings, but the Morrígan was healed. Such a fury has a long memory and little capacity for mercy or forgiveness. She prophesied that Cúchulainn's life would end when her cow's calf has grown to a yearling, and she then shattered the wheels of the hero's chariot. The Morrígan has her final vengeance when, in the shape of a crow, she perches on Cúchulainn's shoulder while watching him die. The Morrígan is said to have been witnessed at the Battle of Clontarf on Good Friday in the year 1014, sealing the victory of the Irish, under King Brian Bóruma, over the invading Danes. After this appearance, she vanishes from records, perhaps to be replaced in Irish myth, folklore and legend by her daughter, the banshee.

Lady Sovereignty, sometimes called Sovranty, is the divine, feminine embodiment of a nation, and this mythological figure survives into the modern world in the forms of national matrons such as Britannia, Hibernia and Columbia. In early times, the concept of such an embodiment was often central to the theme of hierogamy, 'sacred marriage', a rite of kingship in which royal power was thought to be imbued through a union between the ruler – a mortal king – and a divine fertility goddess. In some cases, such as that of the ancient Sumerians, it is thought that the king enacted this union through the medium of a priestess of the goddess, who acted as a sexual vehicle through which the king could mate with the divine. The theme of sacral kingship validated and empowered through sexual communion with a divine consort is common throughout the Indo-European traditions, and is thought to pre-date the Celtic literary records by several centuries. Many argue that such concepts of sacral kingship evolved from ancient cults which linked the sun god's warmth and vitality with the agricultural fertility of the earth goddess. In medieval Irish mythology, the Lady Sovereignty figure clearly comprises the attributes of such a fertility goddess, and the king seems to be a mortal stand-in for – indeed, in some ways the anointed successor to – the sun god himself. In the sexual rituals associated with this theme, one might well argue that both the male and the female involved are acting as the human surrogates of this divine and necessary union. Some records suggest that such pagan rites, sometimes including horses, may have continued in Ireland well into the medieval period. The sovereignty theme, in any case, is extremely common in Irish literature of this period, and often overtly evokes the sexual nature of the union. The concept itself was widespread enough that terms specific to its rituals developed: *banais ríghe* is an expression denoting the 'mating-feast of royal power', a two-part ritual involving the ceremonial offer of a sacred beverage – usually 'red ale' or 'golden mead', again, evoking the light of the sun – to the rightful king from the hand of the goddess followed by the sexual consummation of the sacred relationship. Moreover, a fair amount of Celtic-influenced literature in English reflects this theme, and, far from being unique, Chaucer's 'The Wife of Bath's Tale' provides only the most well-known example of a subgenre of the medieval romance concerned with a figure known as the 'Loathly Lady'.

In the Loathly Lady myth, a young hero is forced against his desire to couple with or marry a grotesque old crone, only to discover a beautiful young bride by his side after he has submitted to the creature's will. It has been suggested that the duality of Lady Sovereignty represents the similarly bifurcated nature of kingship: the onerous and unpleasant responsibilities of ruling are balanced by its seductive and pleasurable powers. Some tales offer an inversion of this theme that takes place at the end of a king's reign: the old man couples with a beautiful maiden, who reverts to a hideous crone, reclaims the royal prerogative imbued unto the ruler by sovereignty, and slays the now powerless former king. The sovereignty theme has clear value as political propaganda, and seems to have been exploited to this effect. Of the many figures associated with the sovereignty theme in medieval Irish mythology, the tripartite Morrígna are among the most obvious, along with Medb, in whom the conflation of sexuality with power is so clearly manifested. The eponymous goddesses such as Ériu are also examples of the genre. Meanwhile, Branwen, the Welsh heroine of the second branch of the *Mabinogion*, also neatly embodies this motif, as, some might suggest, does Rhiannon.

Nemain, the consort of Néit, a war god who appears among the ranks of the Fomorians, is sometimes listed as one of the three Morrígna, generally as a substitute for either Badb or the Morrígan; moreover, the records indicate that Nemain and Badb seem both to share the affections of Néit, further blurring the lines between their identities. As a result of this confusion, Nemain is generally characterized as a manifestation of either Badb or the Morrígan, the latter of which at times seems to comprise all of her sister Morrígna. Nemain's name, however, suggests that she may provide a pale medieval Irish reflection of the ancient Celtic goddess Nemetona, 'She of the Sacred Grove', whose widespread popularity throughout Britain and Gaul is attested by numerous inscriptions containing her name. At a number of locations in the sphere of Roman influence,

Nemetona was linked with manifestations of Mars, the god of war, an association that seems to have survived into Irish myth in the form of Nemain's marriage to Néit.

Medb, or Maeve, is in many ways an embodiment of sovereignty who comprises aspects of earlier Celtic mother goddesses and war goddesses; her seductive allure is manifested in several ways, not least of which is her name itself, which might literally be rendered from the Irish 'she who intoxicates'. It is no great surprise, then, that her name is cognate with the English word 'mead' and the Sanskrit word *madhu*, terms which refer to honey, to the fields of flowers from which this nectar is distilled, and to the sweet, deceptively intoxicating beverage brewed from the fruit of the hive. As though this association between sweet beauty and the perilously potent power it may mask were not clear enough, in the broader Indo-European mythological context, Madhu refers not only to 'honey', but to a Hindu demon; thus Medb's name may link her to a tradition of dangerous deities associated with intoxication. Medb's identity as a sovereignty figure is also recalled through this association with mead, which evokes the holy beverage offered to the king by the goddess during the ritual of sacred marriage. Medb transforms herself at times into a hag, although she is in general described as beautiful and pale, with rippling waves of hair and a long face; her shape-shifting abilities call to mind those of sovereignty goddesses in general, as well as those of her sister destroyer goddesses the Morrígna.

Like the Morrígna, Medb is associated with birds, although the squirrel is also linked with her. The *Táin*, in particular, describes Medb as bedecked in gold and crimson, riding in a chariot like a warrior to the field of battle and carrying a great flaming spear; indeed, these bellicose attributes mark her as a war goddess, along with her capacity to instil terror in her enemies through her very appearance, as well as her lust for the blood of her enemies. In addition, Medb's fleetness of foot, which rivals that of horses, calls to mind Macha and thus Epona. Medb is often said to be the daughter of Eochaid Feidlech, High King at Tara, and four husbands are generally associated with her, Ailill of Connacht being the fourth and the most noteworthy. Some sources attribute as many as nine consorts to Medb, and it is said that her loins offered the only true path to kingship in Tara.

These circumstances speak to her role as a sovereignty figure, bound to each succeeding king through a sacral marriage and sexual liaison, which validated the chosen man's right to rule.

Medb's sexual appetites, which were voracious and legendary, also identify her in more general terms as a fertility goddess. Known as 'Medb of the Friendly Thighs', it is difficult to ascertain the exact number of her paramours, although she claimed to have as many as she wanted, each one vying for her favours in the shadow of another; she boasted that no one man could satisfy her, an accomplishment which required some 32 lovers. Her favourite consort seems to have been Fergus mac Róich, who ultimately dies due to the fury of the cuckolded Ailill, a jealousy perhaps born as much from the military and political ramifications of Fergus's favoured union with Medb as from the rage of a betrayed husband. Fergus himself seems an amalgam of a fertility god of old and a medieval warrior-king whose martial prowess is reflected by his sexual vitality and his role as chief consort to a sovereignty figure. Indeed, Fergus's voracious sexual appetites seem almost a match for Medb's own, and it is said that it took as many as seven ordinary women to satisfy mac Róich's prodigious cravings. Moreover, the very patronymic 'mac Róich' may well derive from an earlier form best rendered from the Irish 'Mighty Steed', a reference to Fergus's massive sexual organs.

The rightful king of Ulster who was duped into abdicating his throne in favour of Conchobar due to his lust for Conchobar's mother Ness, Fergus soon found service in the court of Ailill and in the bed of Medb. After his active role in the events of the *Táin*, in the best-known version of his demise, Fergus died at the hand of Lugaid, a blind warrior-bard whose slaying of Fergus is reminiscent in some aspects of the killing of the Norse god Baldr, who is struck down by his blind brother Höd at the bidding of the demonic Loki. In this, what might seem merely the violent end of a love triangle among mortals takes on much greater mythic ramifications, especially given Fergus mac Róich's own relevant attributes: observing the naked lovers frolicking in a lake, the jealous Ailill made mention to the sightless yet remarkably accurate Lugaid that it gave him joy to see what hart and doe were doing in the water; Lugaid's spear soon found its mark, passing clean through the chest of Fergus and out his back. Perhaps more than any other liaison, Medb's relationship with Fergus under-scores the divine nature of her insatiable sexual appetites, and thus reflects her identity as a deity of the fecund fields; her unquenchable allure to men in general, on the other hand, represents the lust for power Lady Sovereignty incites in those who would woo her.

As the warrior queen of Connacht, Medb is the motivating force behind the central events of the Ulster Cycle, ever displaying an almost irrational hatred of the men of Ulster as she plots their downfall. The events of the *Táin* itself are set in motion by the 'pillow-talk' episode, in which Medb and Ailill argue over which of the two holds sway over the greatest possessions: one night in bed, Ailill remarked that the wife of a rich man was blessed indeed, and this led to a dispute concerning who had brought more wealth to their union. Finally, they commanded that their possessions and riches, from the coarsest and most common to the finest and most costly, be brought out and compared. Again and again, from buckets, pots and pans to bracelets, torcs and rings, Medb and her consort were evenly matched; finally, they counted and measured their livestock – sheep, horses, swine and cattle – and it wasn't until the cowherds brought forth Finnbhennach, the 'White-horned' bull, that Ailill's superiority was established: Finnbennach had, in fact, been born to one of Medb's cows, but the great bull refused to be led by a woman, and thus moved over to Ailill's herds. Medb's fury concerning her husband's possession of a superior bull set in motion the *Táin Bó Cúailnge*, the 'Cattle Raid of Cooley', which concerns Medb's determined attempt to steal Donn Cúailnge, the 'Brown Bull of Cooley', the only bull greater than Finnbennach. Although in other contexts she takes the greatest of Irish heroes as a lover, as one might well expect, in the *Táin* Medb is at first dismissive of Cúchulainn, eventually coming to respect and even to fear the great hero of Ulster. Even in this hero's humiliation of Medb, however, fertility themes are obvious, most notably when Cúchulainn comes upon the vulnerable queen as she is in the midst of the act of menstruating, perhaps the most notable emblem of the goddess's life-giving powers; sparing her life, the hero disparagingly remarks that he is no killer of women. In her thirst for vengeance, Medb sets in motion the machinery which, at long last, will bring down Cúchulainn.

Some traditions suggest that Medb herself comes to a similarly violent end. Conchobar, who was perhaps Medb's first consort, also took each of her sisters as a lover. Eventually Medb turned against Conchobar, and indeed murdered her own sister Clothra (or Clothru), who was at the time pregnant with Conchobar's child; unbeknown to Medb, this son, ripped untimely from his mother's womb, survived. Grown to manhood, Furbaide Ferbend, son of Clothra and Conchobar, struck down his aunt Medb, his mother's killer, with a rock-hard piece of cheese from his sling. Considering the significance of phallic horns in Celtic mythology, Medb's identity as a fertility figure, and the central theme of the theft of a great horned bull in the *Táin*, it is worth noting that Furbaide is sometimes depicted as tri-horned. For this reason, this medieval Irish hero is himself sometimes linked with the ancient Celtic god Cernunnos, and thus the twisted family feud Furbaide brings to its macabre conclusion may faintly echo divine struggles of the misty and largely forgotten past. Although her provenance at least in some measure as a euhemerized goddess seems certain, less clear is Medb's relationship to any known historical personage, though many have suggested that the tradition of this Queen of Connacht might be derived from a historical model. In any case, in later Irish folkloric tradition Medb becomes Queen of the Fairies, and many have claimed that Shakespeare's Queen Mab numbers among her descendants, although the evidence for such lineage is far from conclusive.

In the first branch of the *Mabinogion* we are introduced to a mystical figure named Rhiannon, and it is through his pursuit of her that the Welsh hero Pwyll, known as Head of Annwfn, won the love of an avatar of Epona, the Celtic Horse Goddess. As the story goes, once upon a feast at his court, Pwyll took it upon himself to climb the high mound called Gorsedd Arberth to discover what he could see. The tradition of that place was that any man of noble blood who sat there might not escape that place without having seen a vision or having suffered a beating; unafraid of chancing blows, Pwyll determined to try his luck. From this vantage point, the Head of Annwfn did indeed witness a wondrous sight: riding along the road, he saw a maiden of surpassing beauty, bedecked in gold-embroidered cloth and mounted upon a pale, white horse. The prince sent a messenger to enquire after the identity of the lady, but, although the woman's horse ambled easily along, no matter how fast Pwyll's man ran, he came no closer to her. Returning to his lord, the lad lamented the idleness of his task, and Pwyll concurred with this assessment, ordering the page to mount the swiftest horse in the stables and thus to overtake the maiden, but this, too, failed; as easily as the young woman's steed seemed to meander, it was impossible to gain upon it. When the lad's horse was exhausted, therefore, he returned to Pwyll, who remarked that there was some sort of sorcery afoot. They then went back to court, but the prince was determined to return to Gorsedd Arberth upon the morrow.

The next day Pwyll did return to that high mound, again chancing a buffeting for the sake of a wonder, and this time the young man in his service was prepared with the swiftest mount drawn from the meadows, saddled and ready to race off at an instant's notice. They did not wait in vain, moreover, for soon they saw the same lovely young maiden in cloth of gold, mounted upon her ghostly white horse. The page immediately charged after the lass, but again, although she never did so much as incite her mount to a canter, the boy could make no headway, and she was ever as far away as when he began the pursuit. Although she appeared to remain a constant distance ahead when her pursuer walked, she seemed to pull further away the faster he followed her. Finally, realizing that his foam-flecked mount could do no more, the messenger turned back to his lord no wiser than before. And so Pwyll returned once more to his hall, again frustrated and determined to return.

Upon the third day, the Head of Annwfn again ascended the high mound, this time with his own horse saddled and ready. He was not disappointed in his endeavour, and soon enough the lovely lady appeared in view, mounted and garbed as before, again moving at a slow and easy pace. Although Pwyll leapt onto his own horse, however, the king was no more successful in the pursuit of this maiden than his servant had been, and Pwyll soon perceived that he was unlikely to win such a charmed race. Pulling up his reins, therefore, the Head of Annwfn called after the lady politely, begging her to halt her horse and to speak with him; this the mysterious beauty was glad to do, and she chastised the king in no uncertain terms for punishing his horse with hard toil to attempt in vain what he himself could gain with little effort through courteous words. The lady then identified herself as Rhiannon, daughter of Hefeydd the Old; Rhiannon had sought out Pwyll, it turned out, because she was being forced to marry Gwawl ap Clud, although it was the Head of Annwfn himself that she wished to wed. Looking upon her and perceiving that her beauty put that of any mortal woman on earth to shame, Pwyll was overjoyed at the thought that Rhiannon might be his wife, and they arranged for the wedding feast to take place a year from that very evening, in the hall of Hefeydd the Old. Thus agreed, the lovers parted.

Pwyll returned then to his own man, but of what had passed between him and the maiden he would say not a word, and thus the year passed. On the appointed day, in a party of one hundred riders, Pwyll made his way to the court of the lord who would be his father-in-law. The reunion of the lovers was joyous, and the preparations for the wedding feast were sumptuous; as the revellers sat at feast, however, a supplicant appeared before the seat of Pwyll. This young man seemed noble in bearing and in dress, and when he requested a boon of the groom at this wedding feast, Pwyll, full of the generous spirit of the day, was quick to answer that he would grant any request within his power. At this thoughtless choice of words, Rhiannon was aghast, noting that their visitor was none other than Gwawl ap Clud, her former suitor, who now demanded of Pwyll his bride, his banquet and the wedding prepared for Rhiannon and himself. Thus Rhiannon and the trappings of her wedding feast came into the hands of the man she despised through Pwyll's careless words.

Pwyll was chagrined at his foolishness, but Rhiannon would brook no slur of dishonour upon his name; she therefore advised that her lord grant the supplicant's request, with the knowledge that she had a plan to foil the consummation of Gwawl's happiness. Rhiannon gave to Pwyll a magic bag, the properties of which were such that it might never be filled. She then instructed her love to come again in a year's time, disguised as a beggar, when she would have arranged her wedding feast with Gwawl. Pwyll was to enter the hall alone, but to have his company of warriors poised to answer the call of a hunting horn, which he was to wear about his neck. Attired as a weary traveller, Pwyll was to watch his words carefully this time, as

Gwawl himself would be guarded against a repetition of his own bold and sweeping request. Presenting Gwawl with the charmed bag Rhiannon had provided to him, Pwyll was to ask only for as much food as it would take to fill that sack. The host was sure to grant the request of a lowly vagabond for a bit of sustenance, and when the bag threatened to swallow the entire feast, that host was sure to ask how the mouth of that sack might ever be closed; at that point, the two lovers might hatch their plot in earnest.

A year passed, and all proceeded according to Rhiannon's plan; on the day of the bridal banquet, Pwyll appeared in a lowly state, travel-stained and dirty, trailing a filthy sack. When he approached the lord of the feast with the traditional boon supplication, Gwawl was careful to answer that he would gladly fulfil any reasonable request. His guest simply asked for enough food to fill his bag, and this boon was quickly granted. As more and more provender from the tables was crammed into that bag, however, and it seemed ever just as empty, it quickly became apparent that this was no ordinary sack carried by a common vagrant. When Gwawl asked how the bag might ever be closed, Pwyll answered as Rhiannon had tutored him: that sack would consume all the world until a powerful, rightful king stood upon the pile of food within it with both feet and pronounced it to be full. This Gwawl did, but to his surprise, the bag swallowed him up, too, and Pwyll swiftly tied his rival inside; calling on his horn for his men before Gwawl's followers knew what was happening, Pwyll invented the game of 'Badger in the Bag': each man beat or kicked or struck at the bag with a stick, until Gwawl was ready to come to terms. This was arranged, Gwawl departed, and that night Pwyll and Rhiannon consummated their union. Returning to Pwyll's court, his new bride distributed gifts such as rings, brooches and precious gems to all the nobles whom she met.

After a few years of marital bliss, Pwyll became aware of grumbling among his people because Rhiannon had yet to produce an heir; when he was asked to put his wife aside, however, he refused, asking for another year to have a son with her. Before that year was spent, Rhiannon did bring forth a son, but on the very night of his birth he was stolen away, and the crones charged with watching over him while his mother slept covered the bedclothes in the blood of pups and claimed that Rhiannon had killed the boy in a frenzy. Even when this false charge was levelled at his wife, Pwyll refused to be separated from Rhiannon, although he agreed that she might be judged and punished for the crime of which she was accused. Her punishment was that every day for seven years Rhiannon must appear at the mounting block outside the court of Arberth, and to every traveller she must tell her tale; to every man who wished it, she must offer to carry him on her back into court. Few availed themselves of this transport, however.

Now it happened that the night of the disappearance of Rhiannon's son was May Eve, and that Teyrnon Twrf Liant, 'Great King Roar of the Sea', a liegeman of Pwyll's, fought off a monster which had repeatedly stolen new foals from his prize mare each year on that fateful date. When Teyrnon returned from chasing the monster, he discovered a boy with the foal, and he decided to foster the lad, whom he called Gwri after his 'Golden Hair'. The foal was reared as a steed for the boy, and the two grew up as inseparable companions. When Gwri reached the age of four, however, Teyrnon was struck at his ward's resemblance to his chieftain. Hearing of Rhiannon's humiliation, Teyrnon took Gwri to the Court at Arberth, where the foundling was reunited with his parents. Joyful though she was, however, Rhiannon called the boy Pryderi, after the 'care' and 'anxiety' he had caused her.

Rhiannon is widely thought to be the medieval Welsh incarnation of an ancient Celtic goddess from the misty past who may have been entitled Rigantona, 'Great Queen'. Rhiannon clearly shows resonance, on the other hand, with the ancient horse goddess Epona, and with that goddess's medieval Irish progeny Macha. Rhiannon's identity as the Horse Goddess is emphasized in several telling episodes: of her magical mount which cannot be overtaken; of the colt found with Rhiannon's stolen son (which the same monster that took the lad was attempting to steal); and of Rhiannon's punishment for the supposed slaying of her son, serving as a mount for all comers at the horseblock in the courtyard at Arberth.

The story of Pwyll's relationship with Rhiannon – in addition to providing the context for the birth of the great Welsh hero Pryderi – provides a whole host of mythic and folkloric themes which in some cases illustrate how ancient Celtic themes were manifested in the medieval Welsh tradition. Pwyll's first encounter with Rhiannon at Gorsedd Arberth, the 'throne mound', or 'high seat of knowledge', reinforces the concept of such landmarks as numinous portals to the otherworld, just as May Eve, in the Celtic world, is a potent and liminal time. The couple's conflict with Gwawl, on the other hand, underscores the importance of the proper use of language throughout the *Mabinogion*. The magic bag, meanwhile, into which no end of food and drink may be poured, seems a clear inversion of the Cauldron of Plenty theme, a trope which recurs throughout Celtic mythology, in which it is generally linked with both fecundity and the divine consort of the Great Goddess. Perhaps most importantly to the present purpose, however, Rhiannon's role as the falsely accused wife who is mistreated through no fault of her own links this Welsh face of the goddess with another visage in the same collection.

In the second branch of the *Mabinogion* we meet Branwen, daughter of Llŷr, and it is through her trials and tribulations that we are exposed to the most famous Welsh version of the theme of the mistreated bride. As does the nickname of her brother Bendigeidfran, the very name of Branwen associates this figure with the 'Raven', in this case the 'Shining' or 'Holy' one (*brân* means raven or crow). Although several later Arthurian figures seem to bear related names and may in fact be associated with the heroine of the second branch, one should take care not to conflate this figure with Bronwen, 'She of the Fair Breast'. Branwen was the daughter of Llŷr, the Welsh god of the sea, whom some assume to be derived or borrowed from the Irish tradition's Manannán mac Lir, a provocative thesis in light of the events of Branwen's story. Bendigeidfran, or Brân the Blessed, was the King of Britain; his family included his sister Branwen, his brother Manawydan, and his two half-brothers, the good and kindly Nisien, 'Peace-maker', and the malicious and obstreperous Efnysien, 'War-monger'.

One day the children of Llŷr were gathered along the coast near the Royal Court at Harlech; looking out to sea, they saw thirteen ships coming towards them. In the most beautiful of these vessels rode Matholwch, King of Ireland, along with many warriors, come to seek the hand of Branwen in marriage and thus to build an alliance between Britain and Ireland. Branwen was one of the three matriarchs of Britain, and was reckoned the most beautiful of all women. Brân the Blessed soon came to terms with Matholwch, and agreed to bestow his sister upon the Irish king. The wedding feast was held in a great tent, as Brân was a giant, and far too huge to be able to go into a house. In the morning after the bridal banquet, Efnysien came upon the horses of Matholwch, learned why they were in Wales, and – enraged that his consent for the marriage had not been sought – disfigured each and every Irish horse by hacking off its lips, ears, eyelids and tail.

When word of this outrage reached Matholwch, he made ready to depart from Britain in great wrath and enmity, but Brân managed to assuage the king's wounded pride with a gift of horses to replace his ruined mounts, as well as with treasures of gold and silver; in addition, Brân bestowed upon his brother-in-law the magical Cauldron of Regeneration, and thus they were reconciled. Matholwch then returned in good spirits to Ireland in the company of his bride, who distributed gifts such as rings, brooches and precious gems to all the nobles whom she met in her husband's domain. So a year passed in amity between the King of Ireland and his Welsh Queen, and they had a son together, whom they called Gwern, 'Alder Tree'.

At the end of this year, however, old animosities directed towards the family of Branwen began to surface, most notably bitterness concerning her half-brother Efnysien's insulting mutilation of the king's horses. Branwen's generosity notwithstanding, not to mention Brân's magnanimous recompense for Efniesen's outrageous behaviour, and even in spite of the birth of Gwern, the hatred towards Branwen grew to such a fevered pitch that Matholwch cast her out of his bed and chamber; the queen was then forced to work in the kitchens, and every day the cook gave her a blow upon the ear for her trouble. The men of Ireland, moreover, schemed to keep news of this shame from reaching the shores of Britain by placing an embargo on all traffic between the two islands.

After three years of such treatment, Branwen trained a starling to carry a letter to her brother in Britain informing him of her plight. Brân immediately roused the men of Britain and began an invasion of Ireland. So many were the ships of the Welsh that the Irish looking out to sea thought that they saw a mighty forest upon the waves, with a mountain rising in its midst, its craggy peak high above the tops of the trees. When she was consulted, Branwen interpreted this vision for Matholwch's messengers: what appeared to be trees were the countless masts and yardarms of the British fleet, while the mountain was none other than Brân himself, who was so huge that no ship had ever been built which was large enough to carry him. The Irish fled in the face of such adversaries, crossing the River Shannon and casting down the only bridge so that their enemies might not pursue them; not deterred by this obstacle, however, Brân simply laid himself down over the river and served as a bridge for his army.

Unwilling to face such formidable adversaries in open battle, the Irish sought to defeat the forces of Brân through subterfuge: Matholwch sued for peace, offering the kingship of Ireland to his son Gwern, whereby both islands would fall under the rule of the House of Llŷr; more to the point, as the boy was as beloved to his uncle and the Welsh as he was to his father and the Irish, it was hoped that his ascent to the throne might stave off further hostilities. While this condition was not displeasing to Brân, however, he knew that he could take the Irish crown by force, and so he was not disposed to give way so easily. The Irish nobles, therefore, counselled their king to honour Brân by building him a house. The Welsh giant had never been contained by any such structure before, and it was thought that he would find this offer too attractive to reject. Such was in fact the case, and so the armies came to terms without blows.

The Irish, however, not satisfied with this arrangement, plotted a surprise attack. The hall was supported by one hundred pillars, and on each side of each pillar was a peg; from each peg the Irish hung a sack, and in each sack was an armed warrior. When the Welsh entered the hall, however, Efnysien asked an Irishman what was in each bag; to this question his guide answered each time that the sack contained flour, and the War-monger felt each bag until he found the head of the man within it. Thus he crushed all two hundred skulls into jelly within his mighty grip. The Irish had to suffer these losses in silence, however, or else acknowledge their conspiracy. Then the kingship of Ireland was conferred upon Gwern, and peace compacted between the two armies. The boy king then went to each of his mother's brothers to accept a blessing, and this he received from Brân, from Manawydan and from Nisien; but Efnysien, whose nature was to sow discord rather than to cultivate concord, thought that peace had been too easily bought, and so he thrust his nephew into the depths of the fire before anyone could do anything to save the boy. And so Gwern was consumed by the flames, and the peace he represented was destroyed with him; a great battle ensued, and few in that hall lived to recount the deeds that took place that day.

Only seven men, including Pryderi, remained of the Welsh forces who returned to Britain along with Brân the Blessed, and Brân himself was mortally wounded by a poisoned spear which had struck his foot. Branwen, the daughter of Llŷr, returned with her dying brother to the land of her birth; her homecoming was melancholy, and when she gazed upon that island – and back towards where she had lived as a married woman – she lamented that two great island nations had been decimated for her sake. Branwen sighed in grief as these words escaped her, and she died then and there of a broken heart. Of the vast hosts of the Irish, meanwhile, only five pregnant women had survived, and the race of that island stemmed ever afterwards from the five sons born to those mothers, each of whom chose a mate from among his mother's companions; the five provinces of Ireland are said to have derived from those unions.

Like Rhiannon before her, Branwen manifests ancient associations with birds and with gift-giving that may mark her origin as a goddess. Moreover, Branwen's story also reflects aspects of Rhiannon's, in that both brides are misused through no fault of their own; in Branwen's case, however, the slandered wife is clearly a pawn in a wider political and martial conflict between the heroic pride and military prowess of her ancestral people and those of her husband's tribe. In the despair of Branwen's marital situation – and perhaps most evocatively in her dying lament, uttered with her final breath before a death brought about by the inevitable sorrow inherent in her untenable position – we may hear a resonant echo of the dilemma of the failed 'peace-weaver' bride made so clear in examples, for instance, one might draw from *Beowulf*. The pathos of such a situation illuminates in high relief the medieval mask imposed upon the ancient duality of the Great

Goddess: here the life-giving fertility of the mother goddess is not replaced by the joyful bloodlust of the destroyer goddess, but rather by the doleful visage of the mourner, that feminine figure who has no power but to lament. Like the crone, the constant companion of maiden and wife in the triple-figure of Celtic folklore, Branwen is here associated not with life-giving nor with life-taking powers, but rather with lamentation and the doleful journey to the world of the dead, as she who witnesses and watches over life's passing.

Conclusion: The Identity
of the Goddess

There is one Goddess; her characteristics, her masks and her names are legion. If God is of the sky, this Goddess is of the earth. If God reigns over us, Goddess lives with us. As our constant companion she comes to life in the particular clothes of our multitude of cultural expressions, and often she must bend to the priorities of those expressions. Wherever she emerges, Goddess gives birth to life and she takes life back to herself. She is Mother Earth, the scientists' self-regulating Gaia, who produces Wordsworth's daffodils and the crops that feed us. As the Great Mother, she is the African Oya, the Native American Spider Woman, the Indian Prithvi and the Greek Demeter. At the same time, as Kali in India or Ereshkigal, the terrifying sister of ancient Sumerian Inanna, she is the seductive power that draws us, male and female, writhing in the pangs of love or the agonies of death, into her devouring but welcoming loins. This, of course, is only one understanding of Goddess and her nature.

In this book we have witnessed the emanations of Goddess in the myths of many cultures, in the cultural dreams through which she is revealed. In following those myths as they developed over the centuries, we have inevitably exposed our own development, not only in our particular cultures, but as a species, particularly in the context of our reaction to the feminine aspect of our being, as well as in our attitudes to females in our societies.

In the Goddess as Great Mother, as Gaia or Demeter, or as the Enthroned Goddess of ancient Çatalhöyük, we honour the source of our being, the feminine power of birth-giving, a power that is denied to males. In the Goddess in forms such as the Morrígan or

Inanna, attempting and failing to seduce the heroes Gilgamesh and Cúchulainn, or as Dido being denied by Aeneas, we recognize at once the power of feminine sexuality and the male fear of that power as a threat to patriarchal priorities. In the femme fatale, this aspect of the Goddess takes explicit archetypal human form. In the wifeless deity of the monotheistic religions, it takes theological form. In the treatment of women in societies dominated by men and their male deities, it takes socio-political form. In the myths of Isis, Draupadi, the Virgin Mary and other strong and somewhat mystical figures, we honour what we tend to see as a feminine wisdom based not so much in intellect as in intuition and a mysterious power to transcend the world of reason and science, even to turn death into life.

In short, to confront the masks of Goddess is to confront a biography of a complex being who reflects the manifold nature of the feminine or what our species sees as the feminine side of itself. But this biography cannot be approached linearly or chronologic-ally from birth to death. When we search for the life of Goddess we find a divine child, a maiden, a mother, a wise old crone, a warrior, a huntress, a monster, a seductress and a creatrix. Goddess can be seen as a sacred temple, a holy virgin, a consort of God or as the domin-ant force in the Universe. In sum, Goddess refuses to be defined. The only element that unites her myriad masks is her femaleness. To study her as she is revealed over time is to study our own rela-tion to and understanding of that condition. This conclusion is, of course, disturbing, because it leaves us with the understanding that Ereshkigal, Kali, the Virgin Mary, Isis, Demeter, the Morrígan, Frigg and the Irish queens are all one being, a combined revelation of our collective mind's understanding of what it is to be female.

An inevitable question for anyone concerned with the Goddess is 'where is she today?' Visitors to Catholic, Orthodox and many Anglican churches will discover an answer revealed in icons, paint-ings and sculptures in which the Virgin Mary is celebrated as the most revered of saints. While official doctrine may deny her godhead, her pervasive artistic and devotional use and even such theological concepts as her Immaculate Conception and Assumption and her frequent designation as 'Queen of Heaven' suggest divinity. Mary is said to have appeared many times to favoured people in history. One of her most powerful appearances, as the Virgin of Guadalupe, has resulted in her replacing the Goddess of earlier Earth Mother forms and making it possible for mythologists, at least, to call her today the de facto goddess of Mexico.

Among the so-called great world religions, Goddess remains openly powerful in Hinduism as Devi, or in such forms as the frightening Kali and the nurturing Parvati. In many Native North American cultures, Goddess is a functioning sacred presence as, for instance, Spider Woman, the weaver of creation; White Buffalo Woman, the bringer of laws and customs; or Changing Woman, the guardian of Navajo and Apache girls celebrating puberty ceremonies. A visitor to certain Chinese temples will find worshippers in deep devotion before statues of the Goddess as Guanyin. Animists in Africa worship the Ashanti Earth Mother Asase Yaa or the Congolese creator goddess Nzambi. Finally, Goddess even plays a role in contemporary scientific thought. For depth psychologists she is a sort of triple goddess – maiden, mother and crone – embodying phases in the physical and psychological development of women. In the hypothetical physics of some, she is Gaia, the ancient Earth Mother now seen as our planet itself, reacting to the torments of humanity but adjusting herself to endure, even as her tormentors go the way of earlier, now extinct, visitors to her body. It is fair to say that the Goddess, like this Gaia, is as immortal as any God.

Further Reading

1 The Dawn of the Indian Goddess

Bowker, John, ed., *The Oxford Dictionary of World Religions* (New York and Oxford, 1997)

Gupta, Shakti M., *From Daityas to Devatas in Hindu Mythology* (Bombay, 1973)

Kinsley, David R., *The Sword and the Flute: Kali and Krsna: Dark Visions of the Terrible and the Sublime in Hindu Mythology* (Berkeley, CA, 1975)

Leeming, David, *Asian Mythology* (New York and Oxford, 2001)

—, *The Oxford Companion to World Mythology* (New York and Oxford, 2005)

Mallory, J. P., *In Search of the Indo-Europeans: Language, Archeology and Myth* (London, 1987)

O'Flaherty, Wendy Doniger, *Hindu Myths: A Sourcebook Translated from the Sanskrit* (New York, 1975)

—, *Women, Androgynes, and Other Mythical Beasts* (Chicago, IL, 1980)

Pintchman, Tracy, *The Rise of the Goddess in the Hindu Tradition* (New York, 1994)

Williams, George M., *Hindu Mythology* (New York and Oxford, 2003)

Wnagu, Madhu Bazaz, *Images of Indian Goddesses: Myth, Meanings, and Models* (New Delhi, 2003)

Ziolkowski, Mari P., 'Kali', in *Encyclopedia of Psychology and Religion*, ed. David Leeming, 2nd edn (Heidelberg and New York, 2014), vol. II, pp. 987–9

11 The Religious Conversion of the Near Eastern Goddess

Clinton, Jerome W., *The Tragedy of Sohráb and Rostám: From the Persian National Epic, The Shahname of Abol-Qasem Ferdowsi* (Seattle, WA, 1996)

Curtis, Vesta Sarkhosh, *Persian Myths* (Austin, TX, 1993)
Fee, Christopher R., *Mythology in the Middle Ages: Heroic Tales of Monsters, Magic, and Might* (Santa Barbara, CA, 2011)
Ferdowsi, A., *The Legend of Seyavash* (Washington, DC, 2004)
—, *Fathers and Sons: Stories from the Shahnameh of Ferdowsi*, vol. II (Washington, DC, 2000)
—, *Sunset of Empire: Stories from the Shahnameh of Ferdowsi*, vol. III (Washington, DC, 2004)
—, and D. Davis, *The Lion and the Throne: Stories from the Shahnameh of Ferdowsi*, vol. I (Washington, DC, 1998)
Ganjavi, Nizami, and Julie Scott Meisami, *The Haft Paykar: A Medieval Persian Romance* (Oxford, 1995)
Hinnells, John R., *Persian Mythology* (London, 1975)
Lapidus, Ira M., *A History of Islamic Societies* (Cambridge, 2002)
Levy, Reuben, *The Epic of the Kings: Shah-Nama, the National Epic of Persia* (London, 1985)
Meisami, Julie S., *A Sea of Virtues: Bahr Al-Favaid: A Medieval Islamic Mirror for Princes* (Salt Lake City, UT, 1991)
—, *Medieval Persian Court Poetry* (Princeton, NJ, 1987)
—, *Persian Historiography* (Edinburgh, 1999)
Morgan, David, *Medieval Persia, 1040–1797* (London, 1997)
Nashat, Guity, and Lois Beck, *Women in Iran from the Rise of Islam to 1800* (Urbana, IL, 2003)
Puhvel, Jaan, *Comparative Mythology* (Baltimore, MD, 1987)
Robinson, B., *The Persian Book of Kings: An Epitome of the Shahnama of Firdawsi* (New York, 2002)
Ross, Denison, *The Hafez Poems of Gertrude Bell* (New York, 1981)
Rypka, Jan, *History of Iranian Literature* (Dordrecht, 1968)
Yarshater, Ehsan, *Cambridge History of Iran*, vol. III: *The Seleucid, Parthian, and Sassanian Periods* (Cambridge, 1968)
—, *Encyclopaedia Iranica* (London, 1982). Also available as an online resource: www.iranicaonline.org

III The Scourge of the Middle Eastern and Mediterranean Goddess

Boer, Charles, trans., *The Homeric Hymns* (Chicago, IL, 1970)
Clark, R. T. Rundle, *Myth and Symbol in Ancient Egypt* (London, 1978)
Coogan, Michael David, ed. and trans., *Stories from Ancient Canaan* (Louisville, KT, 1978)
Dalley, Stephanie, trans., *Myths from Mesopotamia* (Oxford and New York, 1989, revised 2000)
Gardner, John, and John Maier, trans., *Gilgamesh* (New York, 1984)
Gimbutas, Marija, *The Language of the Goddess* (San Francisco, CA, 1989)

Hansen, William, *Classical Mythology* (Oxford and New York, 2004)

Hesiod, *Theogony*, trans. Norman O. Brown (Indianapolis, IN, 1953)

Kramer, Samuel Noah, *Sumerian Mythology* (New York, 1961)

Leeming, David A., *From Olympus to Camelot: The World of European Mythology* (Oxford and New York, 2003)

—, *Jealous Gods and Chosen People: The Mythology of the Middle East* (Oxford and New York, 2004)

—, *The Oxford Companion to World Mythology* (Oxford and New York, 2005)

—, *The World of Myth*, 2nd revd edn (Oxford and New York, 2014)

—, and Jake Page, *Goddess: Myths of the Female Divine* (Oxford and New York, 1994)

Pinch, Geraldine, *Egyptian Mythology* (Oxford and New York, 2002)

Wasilewska, Ewa, *Creation Stories of the Middle East* (London and Philadelphia, PA, 2000)

Wolkstein, Diane, and Samuel Noah Kramer, *Inanna: Queen of Heaven and Earth* (New York, 1983)

IV The Battle Lust of the Northern Goddess

Branston, Brian, *Gods of the North* (New York, 1980)

Byock, Jesse, *The Saga of the Volsungs: The Norse Epic of Sigurd the Dragon Slayer* (New York, 1999)

—, *Viking Age Iceland* (New York, 2001)

Crossley-Holland, Kevin, *The Norse Myths* (New York, 1981)

Davidson, H. R. Ellis, *Myths and Symbols in Pagan Europe: Early Scandinavian and Celtic Religions* (Syracuse, NY, 1988)

—, *Norse Mythology: Gods and Myths of Northern Europe* (New York, 1965)

—, *Roles of the Northern Goddess* (London, 1998)

DuBois, Thomas A., *Nordic Religions in the Viking Age* (Philadelphia, PA, 1999)

Faulkes, Anthony, *Edda* (Rutland, VT, 1995)

Fee, Christopher R., *Mythology in the Middle Ages: Heroic Tales of Monsters, Magic, and Might* (Santa Barbara, CA, 2011)

—, with David A. Leeming, *Gods, Heroes and Kings: The Battle for Mythic Britain* (New York and Oxford, 2004)

Hreinsson, Viðar, *The Complete Sagas of Icelanders, Including 49 Tales* (Reykjavík, 1997)

Jones, Gwyn, *A History of the Vikings* (New York and Oxford, 1984)

Kellogg, Robert, *The Sagas of Icelanders: A Selection* (New York, 2000)

Larrington, Carolyne, *The Poetic Edda* (New York and Oxford, 1999)

Lindahl, Carl, John McNamara and John Lindow, *Medieval Folklore:*

A Guide to Myths, Legends, Tales, Beliefs, and Customs (New York and Oxford, 2002)

Lindow, John, *Norse Mythology: A Guide to the Gods, Heroes, Rituals, and Beliefs* (New York and Oxford, 2001)

Page, R. I., *Norse Myths* (Austin, TX, 1990)

Puhvel, Jaan, *Comparative Mythology* (Baltimore, MD, 1987)

Simek, Rudolf, *Dictionary of Northern Mythology*, trans. Angela Hall (Rochester, NY, 1993)

v The Seductive Destruction of the Goddess of the Western Isles

Carr, A. D., *Medieval Wales: British History in Perspective* (Basingstoke, 1995)

Cunliffe, Barry W., *The Celts: A Very Short Introduction* (New York and Oxford, 2003)

Davies, Wendy, *Wales in the Early Middle Ages: Studies in the Early History of Britain* (Leicester, 1982)

Ellis, Peter Berresford, *Dictionary of Celtic Mythology* (New York and Oxford, 1994)

—, *A Dictionary of Irish Mythology* (New York and Oxford, 1991)

Fee, Christopher R., *Mythology in the Middle Ages: Heroic Tales of Monsters, Magic, and Might* (Santa Barbara, CA, 2011)

—, with David A. Leeming, *Gods, Heroes and Kings: The Battle for Mythic Britain* (New York and Oxford, 2004)

Gantz, Jeffrey, *The Mabinogion* (New York, 1996)

Green, Miranda J., *The Celtic World* (London, 1995)

—, *The Gods of the Celts* (Stroud, 1996)

—, *Celtic Myths: The Legendary Past* (Austin, TX, 1993)

Jack, R. I., *Medieval Wales* (London, 1972)

Jones, Gwyn, and Thomas Jones, *The Mabinogion* (New York, 2001)

Kinsella, Thomas, and Louis Le Brocquy, *The Táin* (New York and Oxford, 2002)

Lindahl, Carl, John McNamara and John Lindow, *Medieval Folklore: A Guide to Myths, Legends, Tales, Beliefs, and Customs* (New York and Oxford, 2002)

MacKillop, James, *Dictionary of Celtic Mythology* (New York and Oxford, 1998)

Maier, Bernhard, *Dictionary of Celtic Religion and Culture* (Woodbridge, 1997)

Patterson, Nerys Thomas, *Cattle-lords and Clansmen: The Social Structure of Early Ireland* (Notre Dame, IN, 1994)

Smyth, Daragh, *A Guide to Irish Mythology* (Dublin, 1996)

Acknowledgements

Thanks are due to the Provost's Office and Department of English at Gettysburg College for substantial support throughout this project; most especially, Danielle Dattolo provided key clerical and research assistance, and Jody Rosensteel kept the trains running on time. In addition, we offer special thanks to our editorial assistant and art history consultant Emily Francisco. Finally, we would be remiss if we did not thank Ben Hayes at Reaktion for his unstinting patience, enthusiasm and encouragement.

Photo Acknowledgements

The author and publishers wish to express their thanks to the below sources of illustrative material and/or permission to reproduce it.

© Trustees of the British Museum, London: pp. 20, 24, 29, 34, 36, 45, 54, 61, 64, 68, 73, 82, 88, 102, 105, 106, 113, 118, 120, 121, 125, 131, 136; Los Angeles County Museum of Art, www.lacma.org: pp. 32, 38, 79, 86; The Metropolitan Museum of Art, New York: pp. 6, 86.

Index

Page numbers in italic denote illustrations